A Better Place

A BETTER PLACE
David Selby

QUARRIER PRESS
Charleston, West Virginia

Quarrier Press
Charleston, WV

© 2005, David Selby

All rights reserved. No part of this book may be reproduced in any form or means, electronic or mechanical, including photocopying, recording, or by any information storage and retrieval system, without permission in writing from the publisher.

Front and back cover photographs by Stephen J. Shaluta, Jr.
Book and cover design: Mark S. Phillips

ISBN: 1-891852-47-7
Library of Congress Catalog Card Number: 2005907851

10 9 8 7 6 5 4 3 2 1

Printed in the United States of America

Distributed by:
West Virginia Book Co.
1125 Central Ave.
Charleston, WV 25302
www.wvbookco.com

DEDICATION

This book is dedicated to my ancestors and mountaineers everywhere.

CONTENTS

Acknowledgements viii
Prologue ix
Chapter 1:   Gardeners 1
Chapter 2:   The Lessons of 9-11 11
Chapter 3:   Homeland 27
Chapter 4:   Mountaineers 43
Chapter 5:   "Country Roads" 59
Chapter 6:   *West Virginia Moon* Revisited 69
Chapter 7:   Mountains of Coal 79
Chapter 8:   Those Damn Facts and Figures 99
Chapter 9:   Hometown 105
Chapter 10: Mother 125
Chapter 11: The Carpenter 137
Chapter 12: A West Virginia Doctor 161
Chapter 13: The Other Side of the Mountain 177
Chapter 14: Looking Ahead 201
Postscript 219
Notes and Sources 221
About the Author 227

ACKNOWLEDGEMENTS

This book would not have been possible but for the love and care of my wife and children. The love and friendship of my parents and brother, my in-laws, and the many friends my wife and I made during our time in West Virginia, have been nourishing and inspirational. My wife gave generously of her time, humor, and intelligence while reading the manuscript and offering her welcomed suggestions. My publisher and editor, Bill Clements, and his wife Cheryl, were unerring and most kind with their comments and recommendations. I also wish to thank Tammy Lowers for her warmth and preciseness.

PROLOGUE

My Trip to the Mountains

One Monday morning about 6: o'clock Billy Bebout And I went to the Mountains on this side of Cheat lake Three miles above Fields' Park damn. We got our stuff to-gether in a little cart Billie made from som boards then we started out, we arrived at camp about 11:oo o: clock, the first thing we did was to cook our dinner which we found very pleasing. After dinner we set to work making a "lean-to" in which we slept in when we got finished it was 4:o"clock in the afternoon, then we gathered pine limbs and twigs for a bed, when we got that finished we done some looking around.

In a hour we came back satisfied for we found a nice little place to build a cabin. Then we ate our supper and turned in forgetting about rattle snakes & copperheads.

The next morning the sun came bright and early. We made a fire to cook our breakfast, when we ate I washed the dishes in a small creek about 20 yards from camp. Then we started out, we went to the old stone dam about three miles from the camp. The flowers were blooming and we had to watch out for snakes, for there are plenty up in the mountains where we were at. We keep on going till we came to a revine which hung out over the cliff about a mile from the old stone dam, we came into the large trees and rocks which would reach several feet high. Billy went one way and I went a nother but going up the creek I found the water coming under some rocks and that I could walk through with out my head hitting on the rocks. I considered this the best place I had found.

It was getting close to noon so we started back to camp, on going a short cut I found it took nearly two hours to get back when we got back I was very hungry so we cooked some potatoes for dinner. We ate hardy as if we had hoed corn all day. In the after noon we started to work on our cabin we worked for two days we are building it all out of logs and stone just what we find in the woods. We are still working on the cabin which we hope to have done for this winter for we are planning to stay in it this winter. We are going to do some trapping for coon and foxes. We have taken in one other boy to help us finish our cabin. We all Find it a pleasure to camp in the mountains. [1]

Clyde Selby, age 16, 1932

1

GARDENERS

The faded silver Bronco, air conditioner humming, lumbered down Lankershim Boulevard in the San Fernando Valley of southern California. It passed the Academy of Television and the low rent blocks of small theaters, car dealerships, assorted stores and non-descript apartment dwellings, some adorned with bright banners announcing in English and Spanish the "move-in special." I had never been that far out into the valley, where the sun on this early innocent Saturday morning was already making its heat felt. I drove block after block, musing that the Yellow Pages must be steering me to Nebraska. But evidently, if you wanted bushes, trees and flowers at a reasonable price, you had to be willing to travel. I was in a jolly mood anticipating the plants from Mel-lo-dee Nursery that would soon grace my garden.

My family hadn't been in California long. We had just purchased a house, and I foolishly wanted to do some "back east" landscaping—trying to recreate a familiarity that I was missing. A neighbor had watched me cut my own grass with my own lawnmower that had made the move with us to California from New York, along with other tools of the gardening trade. He said, I think half jokingly, "That's what gardeners are for, no one does their own gardening out here; we're too lazy." The noise of the power mower was forcing my neighbor to raise his voice. "You're embarrassing! Are you crazy, you trying to make me look bad? You're going to put people out of work, people who have risked their lives sneaking across the border so that they can cut your grass, do the things that sane people don't like to do. You want to do your own gardening, move back to West Virginia, wherever that is." I had previously made the mistake of replying to my neighbor's question, "Where in the hell is that accent from?"

My ignorance about California gardening was such that I couldn't understand why I shouldn't cut my own grass. It did seem on a casual survey that most of the yards in my new neighborhood were cared for by Latino gardeners. There was one yard across the street from our house that was tended by a meticulous Chinese gardener. I marveled at the putting green grass he cared for. But cutting the grass had always given me pleasure; it had become therapeutic. It brought back memories of being a boy in West Virginia when I graduated from a push mower to a power mower; I had always delighted in the smell of freshly cut grass.

I've always loved gardening; "putting in" my own tomatoes. My Aunt Zeda back in West Virginia, after I told her that I had "put in my tomatoes," laughed and said it was funny to hear me say "put in my tomatoes." It occurred to me then that I had been gone from West Virginia a long time. "Once Upon A Time" the old song goes. "We sat beneath the willow tree . . . and now the tree is gone. . . . Where did it go?" Yet the longer I was away from the mountain state, the closer I seemed to get. Coming from West Virginia does not mean having a green thumb—in *Iron John,* Robert Bly notes that "good gardeners have golden thumbs." Being a hit and miss gardener, my thumb is neither green nor gold. Planting a garden is a pleasure that many mountaineers enjoy and was one that had been lovingly passed to me from grandparents and uncles. I still feel my grandparents' guiding hands today on mine as I set my tomato plants.

The Mel-o-dee Nursery was an oasis of goodies—I was a kid in a candy shop. Some plants were lush and green; others were adorned with a rainbow of colors. I was hungry and wanted to buy them all, especially those that reminded me of the East, particularly of West Virginia. I lingered over a number of plants trying to make a decision, like an actor carefully choosing his props. The choosing was difficult and time consuming because I wanted one of everything, the right one of everything.

While I was deliberating over my choices, a cheery woman came up to me and asked if I could bring her plants and potting soil to the front of the store to be checked out. I delightedly gathered her plants up and put them in a nursery red wheelbarrow and rolled her plants to the check out counter. A bit later the woman saw me checking out and realized that despite my dress, I was not an employee, and she apologized profusely for her request. "I thought you worked here," she sheepishly laughed, "you look like you could." She could not have given me a bigger compliment. At least I looked like a gardener! I wasn't totally out of my element. I couldn't wait to tell my neighbor. My West Virginia father would be proud. Not only did I look like a workman, my hands would be calloused from doing some real man's work. Earning calloused hands had been instilled in me. I enjoyed physical work—just not too much of it. West Virginia is a cradle of hard work, done by staunch, sturdy and loyal people. Hard, honest physical work was something West Virginians were proud to do. But aren't we all gardeners of a sort, whether we tend a plot of land, our children, a job, our church or a hobby?

Having selected the glorious plants that would transform my arid patch of California desert to a nature preserve reminiscent of my mother-in-law's backyard in Beckley, West Virginia, I headed back to civilization sans air conditioning. The plants were so many they were busting at the sides, their heads poking out all the windows of my Ford Bronco plant mobile, making it nearly impossible for me to see. A few blocks from the nursery, my Bronco decided to take a duster. It was a blistering hot, dry, breezeless day—with no shade in sight—you could fry an egg on the hood. To see what had caused the Bronco to lower its head in surrender without a whimper, I unwisely placed my hand on the burning hood. My jolly mood quickly evaporated. I wanted to kill the Bronco for shutting down in the middle of the parched road in a place not found in any California tourist book.

After managing to get the Bronco hood opened by removing my shirt and wrapping it around my hand for protection, a cloud of steam poured from the engine, as from an old-time locomotive. I spied a group of Latino men standing along the curb—at least twenty of them of similar size and varying ages. They seemed to care little about my predicament beyond a benign curiosity, no doubt having other concerns, like making a few dollars for rent and food.

The Latinos, waiting for someone to come along who will exploit their desperation, had become a familiar sight lined up along curbs all over Los Angeles. They hoped for work on the fly—a random job in a day-to-day existence—day laborers struggling by on a couple hundred bucks a week if they were lucky, like an actor waiting for a role and willing to sell himself cheap. If they were lucky, some homeowner would discreetly drive by looking for cut-rate laborers. Some people complain the curbside Latinos are a "nuisance," that they loiter and urinate in bushes. They form a picture that many do not want to look at, except on days that they want some cheap labor.

These Latinos, for the main, have been forced to leave their homeland because of poverty, politics and, in some cases, war. Life is not fair, but these people deal with it. They are used to it, just as people are in Appalachia—a word and place that is still synonymous with the poor, the underclass, the uneducated, and the downtrodden. The problem is that Appalachia's poor, a largely white population, has been mostly ignored, not even considered an underclass. One thinks of the story Lincoln told about the man who remarked of the skinning of eels, "It doesn't bother them so much, they're used to it." Lincoln went on to the point of his story: "Don't get used to it."[1] It seemed as though my neighbor was right; the Latinos are viewed—and view themselves—as resources to be exploited, not developed. Of course this is racist.

The curb is not the place for dreamers. I wondered about the Latinos' resiliency in the take-no-prisoner sun, though they seemed as tough as any mountaineer and tougher than this one. Los Angeles, I found, could be daunting if you were not sure of who or what you are. Its vastness and emptiness can be challenging. Like many mountaineers, the Latinos' need for education, work, income, and health services was and is great. These men had chosen to think about a future, and though they seemed to my furtive glances indistinguishable from each other, being of similar color, height and dress, you knew that each one in his own way was assuming responsibility for what life was asking of him, that each one was "staunch, sturdy, and loyal." They had something to live for, some thread of hope that had let them endure the suffering I assumed they had faced upon reaching the curb they now occupied.

Some of the Latinos, their faces and arms covered from the

relentless scorching sun in long shirts and straw hats, passed the time waiting for a job by kicking a soccer ball off their high-top leather shoes. This picture brought back the high tops that my mother bought me at Montgomery "Monkey" Wards on High Street in Morgantown, West Virginia. If you wore out the high-top shoes within a prescribed period of time, the store would give you a new pair. I wore out three pairs. The Latinos, with no such bargains in the offing, were still laughing and having fun, ignoring the heat and disillusionment and my predicament. I'd seen men like them in the long-ago faded coal camps of my youth in West Virginia, where poverty did not escape the hard working, where their work was not appreciated by the outside world. Instead the world often viewed them as dumb, ignorant, and lazy.

Los Angeles has become a melting pot. In one local district there are purportedly 100 nationalities. One pre-school class at the Assistance League of Southern California had 19 students speaking 19 different languages, and not one was English. Needless to say, the teacher was challenged. The Latinos reminded me of my forbears and other southern and eastern Europeans—including Hungarians, Italians, Irish, Scots, Poles, Greeks, Jews, and African-Americans—who were imported into West Virginia to work in the backwoods for timber and coal companies. I was reminded of those West Virginia immigrants and the plight of their reality, hearing and seeing an older Latino man standing on the curb, whistling like the lone train he may have hopped a ride north on. Many Latinos, like the immigrants that came to West Virginia, are exploited for cheap labor. They exist at a level where no work means no food.

When there is work it is marginal at best. In West Virginia in the first part of the 19th century, immigrants were often resented out of fear, fear that they were taking jobs away from the locals. Some people back then were unduly worried about West Virginia being swamped with immigrants from Southern Italy, and they made life miserable for those new workers. Today immigrants nationwide are often resented for the same reasons. But this country seemingly requires immigrant labor. Many restaurants and businesses in southern California would find it hard to stay open if not for legal and illegal Latino labor. Not to mention that there would be a dearth of well-maintained lawns.

These people, like many mountaineers, are working, waiting and hoping for a better life. Because West Virginians have lost control of much of the land, people in many parts of the state are basically living in third world conditions. By and large we remain ignorant of the price that is paid by certain people for the comfort of the majority: namely those living under the shadow of the coal industry. But we lament those that we know live under the shadow of poverty, exploitation, and war, albeit as we go about our comfortable lives. The immigrants standing along the curb in L.A., like many in West Virginia today, know things I don't know and may never want to know as they doggedly go about making a life for themselves while doing work that I don't want to do. James Russell Lowell wrote in 1886:

> *The United States have been called on to absorb and assimilate enormous masses of foreign populations, heterogeneous in all respects…of race, language, and traditions…and drawn mainly from that class which might fairly say that the world was not their friend, nor the world's law…and who added to our wealth, and who are ready to die in defence [sic] of a country and of institutions which they know to be worth dying for.* [2]

The United States has been more successful than any other country in being a home for a diverse population. On the whole I think Americans relish the customs and traditions that immigrants bring. Hopefully we will all eventually realize that the acceptance of many cultures is one of the things that make this country, our home, greater and richer.

That stifling midday when my Bronco gave out, some of the Latinos were moving in figure eights among themselves, as though the cement was so hot to their feet that they dared not stand in place for fear death was on their heels. Yet still they talked and laughed at the spot on the curb where they had claimed ownership. As one who prefers a reasonable amount of order, to me their lives appeared madcap and chaotic. I wonder how they can possibly get by in a city that itself feels madcap and chaotic. I assume they had no grand designs other than getting through the day. Yet I detected neither desperation nor despair among them.

Instead I saw joy and life. It was a great lesson. If their dinner was to be beans and rice every night, it looked as though they would delight in it. There is great integrity in any and all work. Still, those lives on the curb are an improvisation at best. But then we all, I suppose, improvise at life. And Los Angeles—to its credit—allows one to reinvent oneself whenever necessary. Just ask any of the many successful L.A. plastic surgeons.

The fumes from the bags of organic potting soil wafting in my hothouse Bronco were going to my head. I was beginning to feel delusional. My jolliness had wilted like my 400 dollars worth of plants threatened to do in the 100-plus degree heat, and my once rosy morning was now closing in with a panicky feeling of doom. How quickly the face of joy changes. The Latinos had certainly seen stranger sights than a broken-down truck bulging with plants out every portal. The paper had recently been full of stories about a group of illegal immigrants forced to watch a man being stabbed repeatedly, undoubtedly fearful of calling the police because of their illegal status.

With the Bronco hood up, I was performing for the Latinos, as though I knew what the problem was when I didn't have a clue. One man sympathetically waved a hammer at me as he went by in a pick-up truck that sounded far worse than the Bronco had, but was still running. If their truck had broken down you would see a couple of them tinkering under the hood and soon they would have it running. How incompetent could I be? I had forgotten the heritage of my grandparents, the heritage of knowing how things work. I watched a boy with a yellow disposable camera around his neck and wondered why he wasn't in school, but remembered it was Saturday. The boy aimed his camera at me. He was the only one who seemed really interested in my dilemma. I waved at him and he turned away, sliding behind a man I assumed to be his father, not taking my picture.

Did I embarrass him? I remembered a time in the rain forest of Grenada seeing several women, a couple with their tops off, washing clothes in a stream. Their young children were playing in the water. It was a beautiful sight. The guide quietly cautioned us not to take pictures. I felt bad that he would think that I would take a picture of such an intimate moment. The truth was I wanted to, but I had seen too many such images stolen from unsuspecting folks in West Virginia. I felt voyeuristic and guilty, yet the women composed a beautiful painting and I could not take my eyes from them. Photographer Shelby Lee Adams, who has made a career out of gracefully photographing Appalachians, would have found a caring, non-exploitative way to capture the women doing their wash in the stream. Perhaps they would have enjoyed seeing their own images, like some Appalachians do once they have decided to trust you. But trust is a short step from distrust.

The Latinos by the thousands come north because they have no choice. My ancestors had that same survival instinct. In the late 18th century they crossed inhospitable mountains hoping for a better life. By the mid-20th century when many coal mines had closed, some of my ancestors went north to Detroit, which was also the destination for my father-in-law's brother. Others, like my mother's sister and uncles, migrated to Columbus and Cleveland.

In the fifties, thousands left West Virginia headed for Cincinnati and Akron. In its time Akron attracted large numbers of West Virginians, so many it was nicknamed the capital of West Virginia. In the 1980s West Virginia lost eight percent of its population. By 1990 only Wyoming had experienced a greater loss of population. During the 90s, West Virginia lost over 10,000 people. Most of them were young, and we lost them to North Carolina[3] down Interstate 77, nicknamed the "Hillbilly Highway." It is still a popular destination for West Virginians, like my cousin Frankie, who are seeking a better life. Some swallow their pride and move to Virginia; others go to Florida. Two people pack up and leave the state almost every hour every day. It is survival instinct. You don't see any potential in the place where you are, so you leave. As my dad said when I told him I was moving to California, "You go where the coal is."

That is what the Latinos do. They will scale or tunnel the highest wall you can build if the motivation and need is great enough. You don't become an actor unless the need is so great that you have no choice. A desperate actor will resort to anything to win a role, for without a role there is no life. It is never about the money—that is until you start making money. The Latinos do what they can to stay alive. They will play whatever role comes their way. The ones I watched that day knew the equation, or wanted to learn it. If caught sneaking across the border, they would try again and again until they got the equation right. This meant how not to get caught, or as my gardener's compatriot said calmly in broken but understandable English upon facing being sent back across the border, "I'll see you in a few weeks." The threat of death will not dissuade him. The word "illegal" means what it means. It stigmatizes them and us. What was separating us? There was the border and the circumstances of birth—I had the luck of being white, but, most importantly, I was born in America—albeit in West Virginia, where people have been shoved to the bottom. Where the trickle-down theory has not been, shall we say, fully realized.

Stranded by the Bronco that mid-morning feeling sorry for myself, I ended up calling my wife, telling her I needed help, that I might have to kill myself. As a friend said, "Anyone worth his salt contemplates suicide." I could see myself, dramatically stretched across the hood in one of my better performances and by the time anyone noticed, my body would be fried. My wife knew how dramatic I could be, and how angry. She knew I didn't want to end up prone in the valley because I had told her numerous times—before my "valley conversion"—that if a truck or stray bullet found me, to get me out of the valley. My wife said, "Call the Auto Club." It was so simple for me, a minor inconvenience. I looked across at the Latinos still waiting like hungry birds for a piece of bread, and knew they probably would never be so fortunate as to be able to call the Auto Club. I thought of my grandparents and what they would think of my self-pity.

That day the San Bernardino Mountains that the valley backs up against were covered with a faded, brown, dirty, lacy curtain of smog. The Bronco episode was one of those moments when I needed the mountains, if only to look at for a moment of contemplation. Later that evening, after being towed home by the Auto Club and planting my patch of paradise, I sat comfortably in my home with an iced tea watching ESPN. It was then that the Latino boy's image with his camera pointed my way would flash, like the green flash that I see at night that my eye doctor says will go away. I've wondered what became of that inquisitive boy.

Today I walk in a mature garden. But the serenity and beauty of the garden is no sure-fire salvation for peace of mind. Nothing can camouflage the misery of others or myself, just as my plants can not dispel that the valley is a desert, and depending on the day, a place of trial and a place of peace.

Illegal immigration, largely Latino, creates a burden on the system. It is an explosive issue that will play out in the political process, a painful and difficult process with no easy answers. Some illegal immigrants are gang members with a wanton disregard for law and order. Others line up for housing subsidies, food stamps, health care, and free public education, though only 25 % attain a high school education.[4] Some were illegally brought across the border when they were toddlers. Some of these illegal aliens have grown up in this country, graduating from college and becoming successful—only to face deportation after it would seem they've earned their place. Can this be fair? Large numbers of illegal immigrants have stayed under the radar and have become an integral part of the communities and workforces in much of the country. In time many of them, like some of the show biz hopefuls that arrive by the hundreds every month, will make a place here—and may even become legal. They will migrate to places like Arkansas and Georgia, Tennessee and North Carolina, maybe West Virginia. They will manage to save enough money to buy or build their own house. Hopefully they will eventually look out their windows and muse that after many stops along the road, they have found a place, a home.

2

THE LESSONS OF 9-11

On the morning of September 11, 2001, at about 6:30 A.M. California time, my wife woke me in tears. For a moment I thought something had happened to a family member. She struggled to gather herself and then told me what had occurred. There were no words to describe whatever it was we were feeling. I felt detached, cold, not comprehending what my wife was telling me. Whatever I eventually said seemed so trite and inadequate that I stumbled into a numbing silence listening to my wife cry. I could not offer her so much as a hug. Then we held each other, wanting to share the pain of the people of New York and Washington, but instead feeling separated, uninvolved, like mere observers. We had protective thoughts of our country, our home, and realized how much we love it. It seemed tragic that so many were paying such an enormous price. Was this really the price of being a country that opens its arms and shelters so many people? Maybe.

During those "end of the world" times, it was hard to think of anything other than getting out of Dodge, circling the wagons and saving our own hides by moving back to the mountains, as my father ever encourages. My immediate thought was that there was no time or sense for law or reason. There was no time for tears. This was an eye for an eye. This was Old Testament territory. We would make them dust. Vultures would feed on their bodies. There would be silence, not a breeze would stir the dark. I wanted to eliminate any threat to my security before the demonic element eliminated me. Then I thought of Lincoln's remark about how when trust is gone, one feels a need to turn violent on his neighbor before his neighbor turns violent on him. "Blood does not restore blood," Lincoln said. He went on to fight the bloodiest war this country has ever known.

E.M. Forster defined tolerance as "tolerating other people even when they don't tolerate you." Forster continued,

> *If tolerance is to play any practical part in the modern world, if any headway is to be made against fanaticism . . . then tolerance must be more than a pious wish, more than a woolly assertion of goodwill. It must have courage, and it must be prepared to take risks.* [1]

This is what home requires, I suppose. Tolerance is very nice but when thinking of my children, I admit to feeling that it's time to balance risks with self-preservation. Today we are on the lookout for danger. Uncertainty abounds at a time when people want certainty, as in airline safety. I have never thought, until recently, about the need to put myself, if necessary, in harm's way.

As the tragic events unfolded eerily on our television screen on 9-11, I escaped to my garden. I had taken care of it, and now it was taking care of me. I'm sure many people were grateful for gardening's attributes in the aftermath of September 11th, whether for simple distraction—simple does not imply simplistic where complexities of life are ignored—or spiritual refuge or as an affirmation of the future. Over the years, gardening has helped me deal with myself and with my fears. As Lili Singer in her newsletter the *Gardener's Companion* expresses, "Every time we sow a seed, it is an act of faith, and each time we water a plant, we…exhibit confidence in the future." My garden was like the mountains of West Virginia where I grew up and where I always felt safe, not at ease necessarily, but safe. West Virginia was home. Home, a true home, is a place without secrets where you can create your own world and space.

As an actor, I have coped with my anxieties and tensions through the world of pretend. Life as an actor allows one to avoid real life. Acting has kept me in contact with my childhood, but it is gardening that has been a refuge for my soul. In the sanctity of the garden that awful morning, I thought of my father and his house and wished I could gather my family and go home to West Virginia. We could make our home in one of the approximately 3,000 caves there, ironically probably not unlike some of those caves where the terrorists hid. We could find an old cave to use as a bomb shelter instead of building one like some folks did in the fifties. We could hide out in an old abandoned coal tunnel. There is the old expression "take to the hills," used when one is in trouble or scared or running from communists or the Feds. You could get lost in those hills, still can, forever if you choose, and people have. When I was a child, I was very afraid of the "bomb" and communists. But Grandma Selby said, "If they ever come after us, David, they'll never be able to find us in these hills."

There was no joy in Mudville, no wit or magnificence, no light, no music, only suffering and sorrow, danger, despair and darkness that horrible day of 9-11. It was as James Russell Lowell wrote of Lincoln's assassination:

Never before that startled April morning did such multitudes of men shed tears for the death of one they had never seen, as if with him a friendly presence had been taken away from their lives, leaving them colder and darker.[2]

We learned that each victim of September 11th had been making his or her way in a chosen field; each had a home, each had a story. We were vividly reminded that each of the more than 3,000 dead was a distinct individual, not just a statistic. We were struck to the heart when loved ones posted pictures of those lost, hoping against hope they would be found. Those pictures heartbreakingly reminded us of the fragileness of life, of life stories that would not be told. The reality of the people lost in 9-11, of being gone when there should have been so much life ahead, is a hard one. They had so much to know and so much to do. What was around the dark corner? What was out there on the other side of their heavens? They had no time to think about being tough, about being right, about being a man or a woman.

We think of their stories, stories that will remain untold because there was no interest before, no time taken to tell them. Fathers and mothers had years to go before reaching the grandparent stage where stories might flow more freely and be more welcomed, even wanted. Stories about how they were brought up, what their parents were like, what excited them as children, what the morning smells were, how cool the air was, what the evenings brought, the mysterious, the gossip, even the first time they got drunk, so many stories that were obliterated, forever lost.

Home was the place so many were desperately and heart-wrenchingly aching for before their end on that terrible morning of unimaginable horror. That was what the young man on one of the doomed planes was trying to do when he reached an airline employee on his cell phone, and asked her to tell his wife he loved her and then asked the employee to say the Lord's Prayer with him. We asked ourselves, "Why?" We all have had so many questions since September 11th. I think of the stewardess on the first plane that hit the towers, who was courageously giving details of what she could see as the plane careened through space, and I think of Annie Dillard's view of a total eclipse:

> *The second before the sun went out we saw a wall of dark shadow come speeding at us. We no sooner saw it than it was upon us, like thunder. It roared up the valley. It slammed our hill and knocked us out. It was the monstrous swift shadow cone of the moon. I have since read that this wave of shadow moves 1,800 miles an hour. Language can give no sense of this sort of speed—1,800 miles an hour. It was 195 miles wide. No end in sight; you saw only the edge. It rolled at you across the land at 1,800 miles an hour, hauling darkness like plague behind it. Seeing it, and knowing it was coming straight for you, was like feeling a slug of anesthetic shoot up your arm. If you think very fast, you may have time to think, "Soon it will hit my brain." You can feel the deadness race up your arm; you can feel the appalling, inhuman speed of your own blood. We saw the shadow coming, and screamed before it hit.* [3]

The last words of the brave stewardess who could think very fast, who saw the final eclipse, were "Oh, my God." For her and all the others, it was a nightmare from which they could not escape. You wondered if the world were on the verge of a giant total eclipse? Some say the world has been on the edge for the better part of the last century and is teetering as we begin this century. After the communists, it was the nuclear holocaust that was imminent. After that it was just plain old detestable ugly power lines and bland food that was contaminated. Now it is terrorism, and AIDS, and mad cow disease, and global warming that threaten the human future, threaten to obliterate all of us.

In times of crisis, Americans tend to come together in large numbers at places of worship to reflect on and pray for those who have suffered. As a whole, Americans are exceedingly generous and when informed will make the right decisions. This was demonstrated ten-fold with the immediate events of post September 11th. Mostly, people's hearts opened up along with their pocketbooks. Compassion demands that idealism and optimism are our responsibility. The innocent face of a young fireman climbing the steps of the tower on 9-11 doing his job was utterly heartbreaking and is forever ingrained on our psyche. That face is the promise of America. It is America's optimism and idealism.

Joan Didion in *The White Album* writes, "We tell ourselves stories in order to live."[4] Those who lost a part of their being on September 11th or in war have attempted to rebuild their lives, tried to find the missing bits and pieces of their life stories. Like archaeologists, people have tried to uncover as many fragments as they can, the sights, the impressions, the sounds and memories as they hope to piece together a story whole. Their memories will be with them always. They will drag them along on their journey and be utterly alone with them and their history until the day they die. They will learn to put up with the memories that hurt, the ghosts of the past, and cherish those memories that made their lives full and rich. There will be surprises in the remains of the ashes of war, bits and pieces that will jump out and bite and others that will soothe and help heal and sustain a future.

Writer Paul Tillich came through the depression and December 7, 1941. He was one of the first writers I went back to after 9-11.

> *There is something astonishing in the American courage…mostly symbolized in the early pioneers. It is present today in the large majority of people. A person may have experienced a tragedy, a destructive fate, the breakdown of convictions, even guilt and momentary despair; he feels neither destroyed nor meaningless nor condemned nor without hope…The typical American, after*

> *he has lost the foundations of his existence, works for new foundations. This is true of the individual and it is true of the nation as a whole.* ⁵

Home is my place in the world, my foxhole, my cocoon, where I can find love, grace, comfort, a semblance of order, and good food. Home is a safe calm harbor amid loved ones for my frets and outbursts. "When we make a home we honor life and we honor all its blessings," wrote Dominique Browning in *House and Garden*, one of my favorite magazines. So many homes in the aftermath of September 11 were disrupted and lost, and to borrow the words of Lincoln, "May they have not been in vain." For those in mourning, I only know to hold tight to your loved ones who live.

On the phone that morning of September 11, 2001, Dad asked, "Is this real?" I didn't know how to comfort him that morning. Our talks sometimes ended in silence, our inarticulateness reared its head, and silence was all we can muster. Later he remarked, "All those people, it's awful hard not to think about them, but we have to go on, we owe it to them. They put all their names on the television but they go by so fast…" There was another of our long silences, and then he said, "Names are special." A little four-year old girl, when told that the terrorists don't know us, replied, "Maybe we should tell them our names." In his poem "Epistle to Be Left in the Earth," Archibald MacLeish writes in a hopeful line to a future race, "I pray you, make in your mouths the words that were our names."⁶ Sadly, when we hear an Arab-sounding name now, often our antennae go up.

I promised Dad I would call him later. I try to be careful with what I promise. For weeks after September 11, 2001, I called regularly to check on Dad, asking how he was doing. "Oh, I'm doing all right, been walking a good bit, feel pretty good." His voice full of concern, he asked after every call, "Are you safe there? Don't you think you should come home to West Virginia?"

September 11, 2001, seemed to open a curtain, and allowed Dad, like many of us, to see life as perhaps he hadn't seen it since before he went off to war those many years ago. People have always fought for their homeland. No group fought harder for their land than those pioneers of West Virginia. Their descendants were

My father in his Navy uniform on 1943.

brought up to believe that something worth fighting for is worth dying for. That is why my father, despite having a draft exempt job, enlisted in World War II, as did most other men of his generation. What Dad and others fought for—risking torture and death—in World War II was the future of mankind, the right of self-determination. Was it all up for grabs? In the aftermath of 9-11-01, a sense of home was threatened for all of us.

I find that I am so American, so baseball and apple pie, and so very much a part of where I came from—West Virginia. I am not, I find, always a nice man, though I like to think in general that I am. In the days after 9-11, I lost some sense of my humanity. What happened to the softness? A woman I know was in our nation's capitol under the dome when suddenly shouts of "Get out, get out!" were screamed. She and others rushed outside. For several minutes she lost track of her husband. Reunited, they made their way to a tour bus. The bus driver drove them out into the Maryland countryside. Along the way they saw smoke from the Pentagon. Ironically, the day before they had had a private audience with a top official in the Defense Department who spoke to them about terrorists, and the threat they pose to the United States. The next day they rented a car along with another couple and drove non-stop back to their homes in Los Angeles, their concept of home forever changed.

How far I thought has man fallen from the Garden! On a bad day you think it is a loathsome age we live in. Decay is all around us. Have we made no progress? Where is the light? This is the area where Paul Tillich holds that the average man becomes "a fanatical defender of the established order… he experiences an unknown depth of anxiety. But if he is not able to take this anxiety into his self-affirmation his anxiety turns into neurosis."[7] After 9-11, it seemed on reading or listening to the news that there were a good many potential neurotics, myself among them, who could smell autumn in the air.

Can anyone be happy today when there is so much anxiety? William Faulkner said many years ago that there is only one question, "When will I be blown up?"[8] What we urgently desire today is a home free of care, free from the anxiety of terrorism. This wish or desire might be considered unrealistic if one lives in the

Middle East, but in the United States? Prior to September 11th, it seemed a very real expectation to be safe, at least in this country. We rarely thought of terrorism as anything other than a movie plot. This level of terrorism was far-fetched. If we are not well organized, terrorism could win out. The fabric of home will be shredded. No home will be safe until all homes are safe.

Home, Kimberly Dovey writes, "can be a room inside a house, a house within a neighborhood, a neighborhood within a city, and a city within a nation."[9] She could have continued, a nation within a world, a world within a universe. In post 9-11, we understand that family is both immediate and extended as is the family of America, as in time will be the global family. But it is globalization that many Arabs are against. We as Americans have had little interest in trying to understand people from the mountains of West Virginia let alone other countries, specifically the Middle Eastern countries. We have not sufficiently fought the perception that America is the great enemy. Somehow they feel or spread the notion that America wants to humiliate them, that the way to avenge this notion is to kill us, and if they die doing it they have paradise to look forward to.

We know now that we must make ourselves understood. We must understand any people or part of the world that hates us enough to be willing to commit the acts of 9-11. It is important for the Muslim community to speak out against the extremists. We must open our homes and not be afraid to enter theirs. The argument that you can't make all homes safe seems an excuse for laziness, irresponsibility and lack of discipline. There is an obligation to one's fellow man. Home is the last refuge for all. In the deep meaning of home, there is no room for dictators, drug dealers, or terrorists, for corporate thieves, corrupt governments, or racists, and on and on in the parade of evil and hypocrisy. Home has no room for excuses, just as home is a place where hope must be kept alive. Home means taking charge of one's life. Education is the cornerstone of home. Each of us is dependent on the other; stranger and friend alike. As a W. H. Auden line relates, "We must love one another or die." In time we will all be one through marriage or some sort of relationship. When this happens, we will find what Aldous Huxley found near the end of his life:

The fact that the ground of all being could be totally manifest in a flowering shrub, human face; the fact that there was a light and this light was also compassion...disregarded in the darkness, the fact of enlightenment remained. [10]

There is immense shock in an incident such as 9-11, but only because we have not been paying attention. People hide behind hope and innocence, not wanting to know. I never paid attention to distant threats of violence that didn't affect my family. I went on with my life, like the people who were lost in those two mountains of offices, or in the trains in Spain and London, in the hotels of Egypt. People the world over innocently living their lives with no anticipation of their fate. I question my own innocence, acknowledging how much I don't know, haven't wanted to know regarding America's dealings overseas. On the other hand, how much does the American public want to know about those things that wreak havoc in our homeland—like absentee ownership of land, stereotypes, mountaintop mining removal, blatant economic exploitation, abject poverty that is worse than any place in the country? How strong is our collective conscience?

Some people in West Virginia expect the worst. There is in them a sense of alienation from the country as a whole. When you live and experience the tragedy and turmoil of destruction, you must feel as though you have an obligation to stay, to see the place through to better times; otherwise you make the very hard decision to leave. Leaving carries a tinge of guilt. Turmoil makes it more difficult to leave—as in Iraq. This country has earned a stake, marked a place, and now our country is marked because of the perception that we are the aggressors. We have dug ourselves a deep hole, we cannot turn our backs and walk away. It was wishful thinking that West Virginia was safe from 9-11. Just finding money for security measures is a problem for the governor. In this day where we are concerned with protecting our borders, I do believe it would be helpful to try and get to know one's neighbors.

Even in West Virginia we don't know our neighbors as well as we think we do. There was the drug case in the poor southern mountains where a homecoming queen was murdered because she knew too much about one family's crack trade. Her murder left people asunder in a community where everyone is family, where a picket fence is commonplace. We thought that a picket fence stands around the borders of our country and the Statue of Liberty was the welcoming gate. Now what? What do we do about strangers at the door?

In southern California, high walls represent a desire for privacy and security. These walls not only keep out strangers, they tend to make strangers of neighbors. Joan Didion living in Los Angeles in the late sixties suggests the mood of those times by telling us she had to avert her eyes from a house blessing verse that hung in her mother-in-law's home in Connecticut.

> *God bless the corners of this house*
> *…And bless the hearth and bless the board*
> *And bless each place of rest-*
> *And bless the crystal windowpane that lets the starlight in*
> *And bless each door that opens wide, to stranger as to kin.*

Joan Didion had Charles Manson and others of his ilk in mind when she talked of not blessing the door that opened wide to strangers. West Virginians, in their early history, opened wide their doors to strangers, and the price is still being paid. They have earned their suspicions, as an old West Virginian exclaimed, "I'm the most cynical person you'll meet outside the third world." A trust in strangers can have dire consequences. Of necessity our country is being careful about who gets through the doors. In the late sixties, my wife and I were living in New York City. One day there was a knock at our apartment door and I casually opened it. A suit told me he was from the FBI. They wanted us to inform them when a suspected drug dealer was in his next-door apartment. Impressed and concerned, we said we would do our duty because that is what West Virginians do if called upon. Our apartment had been robbed not long after we moved in. Our car had been broken into a couple of times.

Meanwhile in West Virginia in the late sixties, my parents still did not have a key to their door. Coming from West Virginia, my wife and I didn't know any drug dealers or other nefarious subjects. We found it hard not to open the door when someone knocked.

Sometime thereafter, however, we installed a metal bar that was anchored on an angle from the door to the floor. The security bar was a hazard when one ventured to the bathroom at night, and was cumbersome and unattractive and awkward to unlock and release in order to open the door for an innocent visitor. It was our cheap version of the "Patriot Act."

On another occasion at our house in California several years later, two men appeared at our open door to check the cable television, which I had not requested. Having been robbed once before at our house on a bright beautiful southern California day, my West Virginia hospitality gave way to suspicions, but I showed the men where the cable line ran to our house. Along the way they saw my horseshoe pit. The horseshoes were there, and as a way of diverting their attention, I suggested they try it. I showed them how to hold the shoes. I was getting ever more anxious and started telling them about West Virginia, how the game of horseshoes was from my youth in West Virginia. I was trying to make friends of them because by now I was sure they were not from the cable company, and I was also sure they knew I knew they weren't.

We played the game out and soon they left, saying they would check the cable another day. I nervously, cheerfully, bid them farewell. They drove away in an unmarked white van, the same kind of anonymous panel truck Joan Didion mentions being suspicious of back in the sixties. Hurriedly I called the cable company, and just as I suspected, they did not have any repairmen in my area. I called the police and gave them a description of the men and their van. The police told me to be alert, watchful, and report any suspicious activity. We hear this advice all too often today. I am now careful to lock the doors and set the alarm no matter how idyllic it seems. I have a "Club" for my car. I insist my wife and children have cell phones and I dream about West Virginia with its low crime rate or Denmark, where supposedly children can still accept candy from strangers.

America has long been blamed, as James Russell Lowell noted back in 1886, for seemingly every new ailment that befalls another country "where the evil example of Democracy in America is cited as the source…and quite as little connected with it by any sequence of cause and effect."[11] It is always said and written that this arrogant country wants to mold the rest of the world in its image. On the whole, it's not a bad image, but it is not for everybody. We live in a mostly open society with our books, our paintings and music, the freedom to shave or not, cover our faces or not. We have been somewhat successful at giving individuals freedom and education while not sacrificing society as a whole.

As far as I know, no one who comes to this country is forced to give up his religion or traditions, although some traditions may be hard to hang onto. When I was a child, I couldn't distinguish between ethnicities; I didn't know Jewish from Italian. My mother's lifelong friend was Jewish. My first girlfriend was Italian. In my hometown, my favorite restaurant is a Mediterranean one. Interestingly enough the main restaurant, now closed, in my youth was owned and run by a Greek family. Today especially because of the universities and colleges, parts of West Virginia are vibrantly connected to a population from nearly every point of the world. Not long ago, I met two women from Iran in Morgantown. After talking, we had our picture taken together. One of them had recognized me from a television series I had been on that is shown in their country. I had put my arm on the back of one woman while posing for the photo. She gently told me that she would not be able to show the picture if my arm was around her. She had not previously refused to shake my hand, though on reflection she had been somewhat self-conscious about it. I had offered my hand in innocence not thinking that there could be a problem for her. I'm not sure where her discomfort came from, but we must respect that. The sex and supposed materialism that we no doubt aggressively sell and buy does offend many we export them to, but they also offend some here at home.

Are McDonald's and Hollywood our image to the world? Do McDonalds, Microsoft, AOL Time-Warner, and Wal-Mart wield more influence in the world than our government? This does present problems here at home. Witness the fights that various communities have waged against Wal-Mart. The mall in Saudi Arabia has some of the same stores as Rodeo Drive in Beverly Hills. Have foreign governments, like some of our cities and towns, lost the control and power to say no to influential companies they don't want?

Can we ever live in peace in an increasingly smaller world with such a diverse people? At the moment the divide is very distressing. Will religious and ethnic conflicts disrupt our ways? Can the United States do anything about them? How will our home be affected? "Remember the good old days?" "You mean the Civil War good old days or the marches for Civil Rights good old days?" Will the pressure be toward more conformity in our society? Do we want a homogenized society that doesn't encourage individualism, but instead encourages a massive herd mentality that social critics already say is too concerned with wealth and celebrity? As a nation, we have welcomed difference; we just have to continually learn how to live with it. We have to be able to make people truly have a sense of belonging to something greater than "making it." Before people dare to change, they want to be convinced that if they do vote for change, tomorrow will be better than today, or at least not worse.

But America is an impatient country. We like instant gratification. If grace is on our side, the so-called "convergence" of communications will foster the good in humanity. Good can come out of the most dismal of situations. There is a light in darkness as we cry out for the wounded souls. It is the people leading the technology of "convergence" that will matter, just as it is the immediate family that is an extension of who and what each of us is. The innocent child endlessly looking out the car window for the expanse beyond must be made aware of what is on the other side of the hill. We all need to be aware of what is on the other side, but we must try and keep the wonder of a child intact. Thoreau mused:

> *If the engine whistles, let it whistle till it is hoarse for its pains. If the bell rings, why should we run? . . . Let us settle ourselves, and work and wedge our feet downward through the mud and slush of opinion, and prejudice, and tradition, and delusion, and appearance…till we come to a hard bottom…which we can call reality.* [12]

We cling to our country, as children cling to their mothers. We know and pray it will not only survive but will be a better country. The young will look back at our country's story and will cling tighter than ever to what it stands for and will take us over the mountain to a place where we will be informed and not be apart or afraid.

As our nation was beginning the assault on the moon, Eric Sevareid, one of the great newsmen, reflected:

> *There must come a time, in every generation, when those who are older secretly get off the train of progress, willing to go back where they came from, if they can find the way. We're afraid we're getting off now. Cheer, if you wish, the first General or Ph.D. who splatters something on the kindly face of the moon. We shall grieve for him, for ourself, for the young lovers and poets and dreamers to come, because the ancient moon will never be the same again. Therefore, we suspect, the heart of man will never be the same.* [13]

I suspect a lot of people wanted to get off the train of progress after 9-11 and go back where they came from. That morning, after 9-11, I felt, as I did when my mother passed away, suddenly old. We would go back to that simpler time—if we could find the way. "Try to remember the kind of September when life was slow and oh, so mellow..." the song from the musical *The Fantastics* goes. September 11th forged a new path. We will never look back without grieving for the lost and tortured families and for a kind of carefree-ness. I feel for the children who will not look to the skies with the same innocent wonder as I did as a child when a plane passed over the house.

How are we going to redefine the world we live in when terrorists aspiring to the heavens of paradise conspire deeds of annihilation? When will man's better nature step up? How do we take the best from each other? What leaders with new voices will open the door to a future that at the moment seems in peril, where time is short, where all our failures are utterly human? I don't know that "convergence" is going to help. It is said that time heals all wounds. I think for fighting men some wounds never heal. We are in a long process, and the transition will not be easy. We do need to think anew about our lives, examine ourselves, and our beliefs, think about our capacity for pity and tolerance and about how our country should respond to the many issues it is facing. Today there is a shadow across the world. Some say it is America's shadow of money and corruption, with self-interest behind every move we make. Our standing in the world community has taken a beating. This resentment, fair or not, must be understood. Hostility is often directed upward and the United States, known as the superpower, the wealthiest, has a target on its chest and that means on every American. America's troubles abroad make it harder to deal with troubles at home.

9-11 changed our lives on so many levels. Those who plotted and carried out the Twin Towers' horror and the other not-so-demonstrative critics who see no value in the American way have it wrong. It is more than just the making of products. It is, as Tillich says, "the production itself." It is the creative process, of building, of going forward—the future. This is part of homemaking. Thousands of individuals around the world were involved with the process of production and creativity when their lives were taken in the name of religion. It was the future those victims were striving for and we are fighting for because if we do not, then all the advances will be lost, and the loss will not just be America's but the world's, for evolution itself will have stopped. This does not mean casual exploitation with progress at any price. America will be a more serious nation. Let it not be too serious.

Will September 11 eventually make us a more responsible and caring nation, a better and stronger nation? It is the best we can hope for from the recent past. Perhaps we will find how to protect our honor and dignity by seeing that truth is decency over indecency, honesty over deceit, hard work over indolence, discipline over chaos and courtesy over rudeness. We all look at life differently now. My travails and anxieties now seem insignificant, though no less bothersome. I do have other things to think about. We all do. Real things. 9-11 made me realize that I wanted to know my father better. I wanted to see what signposts were there for us in an unknown future. The clues would be ever changing, but some answers perhaps would be forthcoming. I went to bed very late the night of 9-11. Strangely and disturbingly, I slept soundly.

3

HOMELAND

There is hardly a day in my life that a conscious thought does not come forth concerning where I grew up. That place is still unknown, though many know part of it. It is a place that is still framed in stereotypes, still the lost island. That place, West Virginia, has sustained me through the years. It was a rural area and largely still is today. I have spent my life, since leaving, in cities. Today, living in the endlessly changing landscape of Los Angeles, I delight in having such a place as West Virginia where I can return for renewal, like a migratory bird, for what I call my pick-me-up visits. The hills, the trees, the flowers, all the smells and tastes of my childhood are still strong. If I see a bird plucking a worm or a hungry squirrel outside my California window, or smell that much appreciated southern California rain or hear an old Methodist hymn, I am taken right back and set plump in the middle of granddad's hay field or a field of goldenrod and laurel as when I was a child. I am surrounded by the blessed hills, those secluding walls—the garden of West Virginia—hills that spread from the central and southern Appalachians, from the Blue Ridge and Allegheny Mountains and the valleys of the Shenandoah to the lowlands of the Ohio. It is a region as old and storied as any.

My place resonated primarily with the beginnings of home, and home was West Virginia. Back when I was a child, I had no idea, geographically, where my state was situated, where my place was. I was not aware of Appalachia as a child. I never knew I lived in it. I couldn't spell Appalachia, couldn't pronounce it, and didn't know where it was. The Appalachian Regional Development, I later learned, included all of West Virginia, making West Virginia eligible for economic largesse from the federal government so that government welfare became a business of its own. It also gave

West Virginia a label, a negative connotation of "illiterate, simple mountain farmers." The joke goes, "Where's Appalachia? Wherever the politicians need it."

One wonders what the identity of West Virginia will be for its children in years to come. How states are perceived in the family of states reflects on the people that inhabit them. We are marked by where we come from, fairly or not. "He's a Texan" can be colored good or bad. New Yorkers are in a hurry, talk too fast, and are not friendly. And we all know how loopy Californians are. West Virginians? Mountaineers? Coal was equated with being poor, of being dirty with lungs choked with black dust, and with being uneducated. People know about hillbillies and the jokes about marrying your cousin. "West Virginia is one big happy family – really!" You might be considered a West Virginian if "your brother-in-law is also your uncle" or "your diploma contains the words Trucking Institute," or "you have a rag for a gas cap," or you know the answer to "if a man and woman divorce, are they still brother and sister?" and on and on.

One of West Virginia's great teachers, Dr. Ruel Foster, wrote about West Virginia: "The mystery lies in the fact that place has a more lasting identity than we have, and we tend to attach ourselves to identity and thus to place." [1] But it is people that create place. So it seems prudent to make sure that we create a place that the children of West Virginia can willingly attach themselves to and want to be identified with. West Virginia is a place that was brought about after agitating for years, a place that was born because people stood up and fought for their rights and eventually carved out—oh let's say—a coal tipple on a hillside and thus identified a place, a place they would come to realize was benefiting but a few political and industrial leaders.

Place is important. As the writer Wallace Stegner commented on the influence of place, "Expose a child to a particular environment at his susceptible time and he will perceive in the shapes of that environment until he dies."[2] I think of the children in Afghanistan. What is their hope of overcoming hatred? What future is there for young girls? Will learning ever be possible? Certainly For as Francis Bacon reminded us, "In order for the light to shine so brighly, the darkness must be present." We may now say that perhaps we are in the deepest of the dark, so the light will be the brightest of the bright. It is hard if not impossible to negate the effect that place has on one's being, one's sense of home. Place can be restrictive and make for carelessness and laziness and can allow us to take for granted that which should never be taken for granted: that our place will always be there.

Until my mother's death, as well as after terrorism was in my face threatening my home, I never paid much attention to place. I hadn't taken the time to learn. I had only the most rudimentary knowledge of the Muslim countries. I was more concerned that my car was running, that my plane would leave on time, never thinking that the research and knowledge it took to build the plane, a plane built for the benefit of people, would be bastardized and the result of that knowledge and research would be used as an instrument of death. There is evil—and judging from the terrorists of 9-11—there is an educated evil. We have to educate ourselves. Sometimes, as it was with Abraham Lincoln, learning takes determination and staying power. We have to educate ourselves about our place. We must know what is going on in our place and other places. It is a requirement for its survival and for our own.

The early West Virginia settlers struggled against adversity. My ancestors left no written account of their lives, so one has to piece together bits and pieces like stones in a stream. What does it mean to find an old soldier's letter in a book or in an attic? Is it just a curiosity or could by chance the letter tell us something of life that could illuminate where we are today? Some will argue that we are better off not accentuating our different heritages, that the love letter in the attic or the Civil War relic on display are of a dead past that means nothing. Some say that we are one people with no borders and the sooner we can arrive at a world of a true multi-racial nationality of people, the better we will be.

When children become adults and are searching for something, a sense of home, they tend to look back or are thrown back to their childhood, hoping to find some clues. I seem to do nothing but look back for something that is not readily there. I must trust that it is not lost, that I will remember bits and pieces that surely have followed me along my path. My father will, in a treasured moment, recall with clarity some name or tale. These things will

The author with his Grandmother Selby.

add up, and hopefully I will understand them and pass them on like genes to my children so that they may have a fuller home. We all bring the baggage of childhood into adulthood. The problem is that nothing is as it was, nor is its memory, but that doesn't stop the urge or the need to look back. When one thinks of the future, one may prefer the past. We don't seemed to have improved much on the past in terms of wanting to destroy each other. There are days you need to tune out the news, to not have to think about what is going on in the real world. And what is real?

My journeys back to the place where I'm from is a necessary part of my being. For many years, I thought of West Virginia simply as the place where I was raised. I was and am pleased to visit and feel comfortable and content when I do. I feel cradled in those hills—refreshed, cleansed, re-encouraged, reinvigorated, and if time didn't stand still, it at least seemed to for me whenever I was back there. It was and is a place where I could still feel the history, hear its original voice, relearn the good lessons from the past, and re-appreciate the traditional values of work, love, and honor. West Virginia is at once inviting and forbidding in its mystery; I always felt a part of something there, and proud of it. But it was only after I had left West Virginia before I began to glimmer a sense of the place, its conflicted history, to appreciate the treasures of this secret place and its people—treasures that I have carried with me in my travels and have been a significant part of my home.

We are all individuals, and wherever we come from is as important to our individuality as our names. As a young man, I had never considered the idea that where I came from had any effect on who or what I was. Even my wife, who has no desire to ever move back to West Virginia, admits that it's nice to return and leave with a better sense of who we are. Although I have been ever returning since my wife and I left in our youth, and though we have tried to "give back" in whatever way we can—enjoying the process and being rewarded ten-fold—I had not taken the time to reflect on what the place and its people have meant to me, what they have given me.

I am eternally grateful for the place and to my ancestors. I was nervous of leaving home, afraid of living, of dying. After marrying my wife, I was ready to move on and experience change.

It was folly, however, to think that the hills that I had walked as a child had had no influence on me. West Virginia was proudly ingrained in my pores—even the way I walk or lope, the way I lean like a tall thin locust tree that the wind has its way with, is somehow West Virginian. It is my history. It is in my blood, the nature of my being. It is in the common bond I share with the many friends we have there. Being from West Virginia binds us together. West Virginia enabled me with my wife's unwavering support, despite my, at times, paralyzing fears, to move forward, and build a life, a home. Considering all, it seems inevitable that I would have been born in West Virginia and that I would become an actor.

Family ties are more tenuous now. The Muslims feel America's family structure is at odds with what they desire. Perhaps the terrorists see this as a weakness to be exploited. Hard lives can take their toll on family. It is harder if not impossible to maintain the close-knit family of yesterday. We are fortunate if we get to catch glimpses of a parent in the environment of their own childhood, especially when it is a childhood that for whatever reasons the parent does not wish to revisit. My parents rarely reminisced in my company about their childhoods or when they met or married or about any kind of story they shared. There are a precious few pictures of them when they were young and together. There's not so much as a note or card between them during Dad's courtship of the coal miner's daughter. There are no letters from him when he was in the Navy during WWII. There is no wedding certificate, and as far as I know, they never celebrated a wedding anniversary until my brother and I gave them a 50th anniversary party.

West Virginians are noted talkers and storytellers. There is a strong oral tradition with myths, poetry and ghost stories. But my family was non-verbal. There must have been family stories in the farm land of Pleasant Hill, and the coal camps of Brady, and Everttsville, West Virginia, but none were passed on to me. So there were no stories that I could pass on to my children. I don't recall a single story being told by anyone from either side of my family. None of my ancestors were writers either. And my father's side was English—noted for the written word. I don't know of a single letter from any of my ancestors on either side of my family.

There were no pictures of long-gone relatives and precious little talk of ancestors, no songs we sang together, no family traditions, and we attended few reunions. There were no books and no phantom of the opera lurking behind a ghostly past in the attic of my childhood. While music is an Appalachian mainstay, I don't know of any old songs ever being sung or any musical instrument ever being played by anyone. Not even a bagpipe from my mother's Scottish father. My family seems to have been totally devoid of any musical talent, and my attempt at the trombone is proof of the pudding. At Morgantown Junior High, bandleader Mr. Paul Pickard said I had the lips to play the trombone. Lips do not a trombone player make.

My ancestors did not talk about the past. They were too busy getting on with life, especially after World War II, to ponder the past. For my mother, the past was something to forget about. But my parent's childhood had a residual effect on my brother and me. I had never given any thought to my family tree. "Where do you come from?" "Where were you raised?" "Where's home?" Then a stranger found me one day and said we were related. He was tracking our genealogy and sent me a picture of a man named Howard Selby in England, an actor none-the-less, who looked remarkably like my father. While not perhaps too unusual, this was very intriguing and started me thinking about my place. For the first time, I began to ponder a little about where I had come from, my bloodlines. And why did I feel this rather intense relationship with a place that I had long since left?

Even if you had nothing in your attic, no old magazines or newspapers, or books to guide you, no passed-down stories or family history, even if you had no interest in the past whatsoever when you were young because you were too busy being a kid, eventually you found that place was important because you couldn't get away from it nor did you want to. My attachment to the land and mountains of West Virginia was like those of others. Out of the hills, I felt somewhat exposed. The longer I was away the more complicated my life seemed to get, the very thing that West Virginians seek to avoid and one reason why they stay in the hills.

It is important to learn one's past because it can be a building block for home. The past offers up our limitations and teaches us compassion for those West Virginians who have suffered mightily for others' comfort and convenience. As Lincoln said about slavery, "you work and toil and earn bread, and I'll eat it." There is no chance to see all of a past, even your own; but with some luck, you can see enough to piece together ruins as an archaeologist does. Until one begins this eternal search, one is in a state of flux, and, at its worst, personal chaos.

It was the turmoil of the Civil War that propelled the Mountain State to break away from Virginia. The people in the mountains did not wish to secede from the Union. They all shared a spirit and a willingness to fight and thus saved the Union from dissolution. It is worthy to note that the vote on the ordinance of secession from the Union in the counties that now comprise West Virginia was 4,000 votes for secession and 44,000 against.

Many years before the Civil War, there had been dissatisfaction on the part of those in the counties of Virginia west of the Allegheny Mountains. People felt that they were not equals. They felt they were not getting their fair share from genteel Virginia, that taxes favored the eastern part of the state, and that all the wealth and power was to the east. Commerce between the two areas was very difficult. There was no way to get to the west except on horseback. People took paddle flatboats to Pittsburgh via the Ohio and Monongahela Rivers. Well over a century later it was instilled in me in a fifth grade West Virginia history class that we had been victims of Virginia's exploitation. As it happens that would pale in comparison to the continual exploitation by the coal and timber industries, where people were tricked or pressured and forced to give up their land rights.

The early mountaineers rightfully felt cheated. How about present day mountaineers? Back when statehood was brewing, there were no canals or public works. Slavery was not successful in the mountains and hadn't gained a foothold, so slave holding was not a profitable venture. There were no plans to improve the state of life for the hill people aside from the one time state hospital—insane asylum—at Weston, a rather grand hand-cut stone building erected in 1860. Virginia probably thought those "mountaineers" needed someplace fine to be put away. The bitterness continued and finally reached a point where the mountaineers were riled enough to form their own state. After Virginia seceded, the reorganized state of Virginia was convened and voted that the mountaineers could indeed form their own state. So with courage, tears, heart, and joy combined with the leadership of both Lincoln and a group of mountaineers led by Francis Pierpont, the mountaineers formed a new state. Democracy was saved. It is of interest that Francis Pierpont was one of the charter members in 1853 of the Monongahela Mining and Manufacturing Company, which was a precursor of the absentee-owned Consolidation Coal Company for whom many mountaineers worked as coal miners. During ceremonies in Statuary Hall at the unveiling and presentation of Francis Pierpont's statue, he was described as having "had a high and unflinching integrity, personal and political, which flattery could not cajole and no temptation could seduce. He would neither do wrong himself nor tolerate it in those around him." I trust this was true and that the business leader was not motivated by self-profit.

Lincoln, after much thought and consideration during the midst of the war, signed West Virginia into statehood on December 31, 1862. West Virginia is the only state to have the honor of being designated by presidential proclamation. West Virginia didn't officially become a state until June 20, 1863. Interestingly, while admission to statehood was approved by the reorganized Virginia legislature, not all of the qualified voters chose to vote. Lincoln wrote, "...it is not the qualified voters, but the qualified voters who choose to vote, that constitute the political power of the state." Choose to vote, West Virginians! On a shelf in our house sits a coal miner crafted from coal, a fitting use for coal. This sculpture sits beside another coal sculpture of Lincoln's boyhood home which seems fitting because Lincoln had more in common with the hill people of western Virginia than he did with those in the lowlands and gently rolling hills around Richmond. Lincoln would have been one with the West Virginia people even though he didn't have the greatest sympathy for external circumstances that hold people back. Lincoln held that:

> *the value of life is to improve one's condition. Whatever is calculated to advance the condition of the honest, struggling*

laboring man, so far as my judgment will enable me to judge of a correct thing, I am for that thing.[3]

In the fifth grade I, along with most West Virginia children, had a class called West Virginia History. It was there that I learned that President Lincoln was the one who made West Virginia a state—largely for political reasons. West Virginia's birthday of June 20, 1863 was more important to me than my own birthday. Our family was not big into family birthday celebrations, but every year during my growing up the papers and classrooms were adorned with articles and pictures commemorating West Virginia's founding. I learned the physical shape of our state and its boundaries. In 1863 when borders were being drawn, Buchanan County was left in Virginia because the makers of West Virginia reportedly did not want a third panhandle jetting southward like the state's other panhandles that sprouted northward and eastward—a good decision—aesthetically at least.

There was a time when I could name all fifty-five counties with their county seats. I could name all the rivers, the native trees, the birds, the animals, and the state flower. I collected pictures of them all. I pressed the leaves from the trees in a book. I read about Harpers Ferry and John Brown and was captivated by the story of "Stonewall" Jackson who was born in what became West Virginia, but fought with the Confederacy. Many western Virginians fought with the rebels, but more, 40,000 or so, fought with the Union. In some cases it really was brother against brother.

It seemed we studied almost everything about West Virginia in that fifth grade class. We were taught that natural gas, oil, coal and timber—the sycamore, poplar, oak, walnut, maple, and ash trees—were our important resources. They still are, along with cattle, hogs, salt and iron. Today it is also poultry, feed and fruit. I knew about the Baltimore and Ohio Railroad that entered the state at Harpers Ferry and went to Wheeling in 1853 and later, 1857, to Parkersburg. I collected, and still have, pictures of trains, though then I had no understanding of the power plays of the railroads and industrialists. We weren't taught the rather sordid and sorry side of West Virginia's history. Still, when we finished the state history class and each student had their West Virginia History

My Grandma and Grandpap Selby.

book, we were proud, confirmed, certified and stamped first class West Virginians with a child's innocence that claimed the state as our own. The place was sacred. The story of West Virginia is no longer so romantic.

As a West Virginian it seems appropriate that I became a student of Lincoln. I had put a copy of Lincoln's Gettysburg Address into a scrapbook when I was in the ninth grade. But it wasn't until graduate school at Southern Illinois University that I became immersed with Lincoln's life and his writings. As a student actor, a little luck plus my height let me be chosen to play Lincoln. During two summers I undertook the role of Lincoln in two plays: E. P. Conkle's *Prologue to Glory* and a then new play entitled *Mr. Highpockets*. The plays were performed at New Salem. It is now a state park with a reconstructed village of Lincoln's time, where Lincoln lived as a young man.

The town of Petersburg is nearby. Lincoln surveyed the town. Petersburg is a short drive to Springfield where Lincoln lived as a politician and lawyer. It became my passion to trace Lincoln's path through the Illinois countryside and to read as much as I could about Lincoln. Later I undertook to read all that he wrote. Though I have questions about Lincoln's dealing with slavery, I happen to agree with Mario Cuomo when he writes: "What appealed to me most about Lincoln . . . was his lucidity, the sureness of his logic, the cogency of his analysis, and the apparent reasonableness of his conclusions."[4] It was all these attributes and more, including what he meant for West Virginia, that has made my life richer and wiser. Lincoln has been a constant resource for me.

West Virginia's formation was unique and, yes, despite my frustration and anger, still a romantic and vibrant story. It is a story that many in the state are familiar with, but it should be a story, warts and all, that all of America—and especially West Virginians—should know. It is a story of how the practical demonstration of Lincoln's words, "government of the people, by the people, for the people" can go awry. It is a story filled with so much wisdom, tenacity, courage, determination and leadership that it should inspire every West Virginian and ideally instill in us that anything is possible, no matter how far up the hollow one happens to live.

On the other hand, these same children will one day learn that they are at the mercy of a system that is bankrupt and corrupt. It is a system where the blame for the failure to succeed economically is placed on a lack of education and ambition, instead of the constant strangulation from absentee landowners that puts the state in continual economic hardship. The message that is sent seems to be that people in the hills deserve what they get and that they should be thankful for providing cheap energy. West Virginia mistook the founding of the state for freedom, much like the slaves mistook Lincoln's proclamation of freedom.

The current national rankings tell us that there is truth in the perception of poor uneducated families in grim places. Coal companies and others thrive on this perception. They like to fuel the reputation of West Virginians as exotic and ignorant, a sort of a subspecies—nobodies. It absolves them of any guilt. They gain power over the people and that makes it easier to abuse and exploit them. It seems as though there has been a forfeit of responsibility of those in power to step up to the plate and make decisions that would benefit the people. But each one of us has to go to bat for each other and ourselves. I don't mean that we all must—like Lincoln—pull ourselves up by our own bootstraps. There is no easy generalized answer or path to follow in order to free those who feel like they are at the bottom in the hierarchy. The struggle for West Virginians continues today. Lincoln wrote:

> *The eternal struggle between these two principles—right and wrong—throughout the world. They are the two principles that have stood face to face from the beginning of time; and will ever continue to struggle. The one is the common right of humanity and the other the divine right of Kings…. No matter in what shape it comes, whether from the mouth of a king who seeks to bestride the people of his own nation and live by the fruit of their labor, or from one race of men as an apology for enslaving another race, it is the same tyrannical principle.*[5]

It is interesting to note that the enslaved, the exploited, and oppressed race in West Virginia is largely white and their poverty largely ignored.

The pride and the danger that the pioneers risked in establishing the new state of West Virginia cannot be overstated. They created a home out of love and responsibility. They have little relation to the greedy railway men and coal barons, who gave reason for some to feel that the separation from Virginia was a mistake. L.T. Anderson, the late editor of the *Charleston Gazette*, wrote: "If we had remained with Virginia, the coal industry would not have acquired absolute power over land, government and individual lives in the early part of the century."[6] That perhaps is true but there is no way western Virginians were going to be anything but "Mountaineers."

It is ironic that the only change on this country's map as a result of the Civil War was the formation of West Virginia. So yes, Virginia, there is a West Virginia. "Mountaineers," have been trying for generations to get away from Virginia. We're still trying. Whenever I'm asked where I am from and answer, "I'm from West Virginia," I am not surprised to hear, "I've been to Richmond." A few years ago my wife took her seat on a tour bus in Atlanta beside a woman who noticed her accent and asked her where she was from. My wife answered, "West Virginia." The woman yelled to a friend seated far back in the bus "Hey, Jean, I told you there was a West Virginia! That's where this lady's from." Well, that lady, along with many others, needs a geography lesson.

West Virginia is known, by apparently few, as the southern-most northern state and the northern-most southern state and is dotted with both Yankee and Confederate cemeteries. Can you name the five states surrounding the island of West Virginia? West Virginia is not the east, not sophisticated enough. We lack society and have no real knowledge of money, especially "old money." Go over to the Eastern Panhandle of West Virginia and, some will say, you're not really in West Virginia. When West Virginia was granted statehood, two counties—Jefferson and Berkley—wanted nothing to do with the new state. The people of those counties were more closely aligned with old Virginia than they were with the new state and its mountains. They went to court but the Supreme Court ruled that both counties would remain part of West Virginia, a ruling that still rankles some. The Eastern Panhandle is nice country with nice people who don't particularly identify with Appalachia. But then true mountaineers don't often visit the Eastern Panhandle, careful to avoid being contaminated by eastern gentility.

West Virginia is not the south because it's not gentle enough, aristocratic, or graceful enough; it's too hardheaded. There are no southern "dandies" in West Virginia. If there ever were any, they were run out. West Virginia is not only geographically isolated from the mother state, but also socially and economically. There was perhaps an aristocratic attitude toward the hill people, "the peasants." Perhaps there still is a residue of that feeling or perhaps we just like perpetuating that underdog status. The southern mountains of West Virginia corner the entryway to the Southern aristocracy of Charlottesville, Virginia. If a mountaineer wants or needs a dose of aristocracy, he or she must dip down into Virginia and points south.

West Virginia is not the north because no one ever thinks of it as north. They don't want us, and we don't want them. Finally we are not the west, though New Yorkers may hazard a guess that West Virginia's got to be... out west somewhere. I suppose that when Daniel Boone crossed the Blue Ridge he thought he was in the west, and you can make a case for it. A westerner may claim everything west of the Allegheny Mountains. A New Yorker may agree with him. If anyone can claim us, it would be the west. But they could drop all of West Virginia into the Grand Canyon and not think twice about it.

West Virginians have little excuse for not knowing their state's history because Jim Comstock, late publisher of the *West Virginia Hillbilly,* as I recall gave books on the state's history to every county. At one time there was talk of changing the state's name. The name change idea was an attempt to clear up the confusion and be rid of "Virginia" and its southern gentry once and for all. There was some talk of changing the name to "Lincoln" or "Kanawha." I'm glad the name change idea didn't take root. We have fought mightily for our identity, to be able to say with pride and gusto; "West by God, Virginia."

4

MOUNTAINEERS

I am a mountaineer—West Virginia born. My ancestors and others like them were frontiersmen, as independent and patriotic as they come. They were undaunted and optimistic. Most West Virginians, including my ancestors, are descendants of pioneer families who came from Scotland, Ireland, England, and Wales in the 17th and 18th centuries. West Virginians still have closer ties to the traditions, speech, and way of life of early America than anywhere else in the nation. James Selby and William Selby, Sr., were perhaps indentured servants out of a debtors' prison in England, somewhat of a disappointment since we were hoping for a little royalty. [1] That's the danger in looking back; you never know what you'll find, maybe even an actor. They arrived in this country in the mid to late 1600s on the ship *Alexander* and settled in Calvert County, Maryland. Eventually my great-great-great-grandfather, Magruder Selby, in the late 1700s, came into what is now West Virginia, probably by following an old Cherokee path. It may have been one used by Washington and his troops going west over the Allegheny Mountains.

Dad tries hard to hang on to the faint memory of his great-grandparents as told to him by his grandmother, Carrie, who was born in 1853. She told him about bears and mountain lions, and how their family existed on deer and bear meat. His great-grandfather James was born in 1801, and his grandfather Amos was born in 1853. Magruder Selby settled near the western base of Cheat Mountain, and conquered land in the Union district at Pleasant Hill, in what is now Monongalia County. A part of that land is still in the family today. The white clapboard farmhouse was moved in the early 1900s board by board and reconstructed from its pre-Civil War base, to the land where it sits today.

The very land and terrain required individualism, as it was not conducive to wide cultivation or travel. There were no railroads, no roads, and the life in these sparsely settled mountains was starkly different from eastern Virginia. The hills were many, the soil not great, and the weather hard. The people had to be tough. They did their own work with their own hands. Taming the wilderness was the thing that had to be done for survival. The notion that wilderness was being sacrificed and quickly consumed was not of their concern. They were struggling for their lives, lives that must have seen their share of dark moments. There was nothing refined in their dress or manner. They had no rank or prestige. They were wild enough to be alone and free.

These settlers were courageous, enterprising men and women who later joined the chorus of dissatisfaction with Virginia and led the next generations to push for statehood and more frustratingly for internal improvements—improvements which were wrongly assumed would follow the industrial awakening. For my dad's family, the farm where the ancestors staked claim was strictly used for my ancestors' own survival. They were not exchangers of goods, were not dependent on the market. As a consequence, although self-sufficient, they were relatively poor, but nothing like the families in the coal camps of my mother's youth where they really were subjects of a colonial master.

Rugged individualism and courage were part of the saga of coal miners throughout West Virginia. These early pioneers were all seeking a home, a place to call their own. They stuck together, looked out for each other, knowing that all they had was each other and a shared harmony with the mountains. These roots of family are present today in West Virginia connecting people to the past and to the mountains, helping them shape their futures—ironically, futures that for many today are outside those mountains.

Another settler who came over the mountains into what is now West Virginia was Daniel Boone, a hero and explorer, who was independent to a point while serving the interests, as Wallace Stegner notes, of speculators and capitalists. It is fitting that Boone settled for a time in western Virginia, a place that once was as natural as he was. He and his family lived for a time around what is now Charleston. He was elected a delegate from that area to the

Virginia Assembly. Later, trying to keep a step ahead of civilization, Boone moved west to Kentucky. As his legend grew, he became the role model for many young boys, myself included. We all wanted coonskin caps. As Stegner says of Boone, he was in myth larger than life. Boone was self-reliant, an expert tracker, an excellent shot, a fierce enemy, the best friend you could have and the soul of chivalry.[2]

I just assumed that Boone the frontiersman and not the coal miner or farmer was the model for West Virginia University's mascot, the Mountaineer—complete with buckskin, coonskin cap and long-shot rifle. The early "mountaineer" was dressed in a lumberjack's plaid shirt and corduroy pants, but this was later traded in for buckskin, which was probably more in tune with original mountaineer attire.[3] Later I learned that the model might have, in fact, been one Eli "Rimfire" Hamrick of Webster County. A statue of this mountaineer was unveiled in 1912. The "Mountaineer" mascot is for some I suppose somewhat of a costumed Hollywood character, a stereotype no less, but for most, the "mountaineer" is a reminder of the culture and tradition, the freedom, spirit, independence, and resiliency that taught West Virginians how to live with dignity and nobility. The "mountaineer" is of the people, representing the entire state—beloved, yet solitary and self-reliant.

Jim Comstock noted that who West Virginians are and why they are that way, "is best described by our state's motto 'Mountaineers are always free.'" But this motto wrought from the most difficult and trying of times, rings false when you look at the state's bottom of the barrel rankings. If you can't read, you can't be free. It is only education that can trump politics. If you can't afford medical care, you can't be free. If you have no transportation, you can't be free. If you're hungry and unemployed, you can't be free. If you have few prospects for self-improvement, you can't be free. If you are carrying a label, you can't be free.

West Virginia's mythical isolation has worked against the people and continues to do so. We West Virginians like to believe we are hidden from all the hustle and bustle, but we get a little offended when nobody knows where we are. A hundred and fifty years ago businessmen from Philadelphia, Pittsburgh and New York had no trouble finding the state when there was money to be made. Business-savvy, down home Armani suits will find West Virginia if they sense a money making opportunity. Not that long ago West Virginia Water Company was bought by a German firm. West Virginia has a quantity of good water that has not been tainted by coal or oil—especially in the Eastern Panhandle. Heck, the eastern states could make a water grab. They could build a water pipeline to New York. A bill was recently passed that will hopefully assure sovereignty of the state's waters for the people. Perhaps a lesson was learned from the fate of the state's coal and timber. Former Governor Wise took a strong stance against weakening West Virginia water quality standards. Despite his efforts, today increased manganese and aluminum are allowed, further reducing water quality.

In the early days, because West Virginia was off the beaten path, there was not a lot of European culture—not many outside influences. Eventually people started white-water rafting down the New River and rock climbing and mountain biking. The lucky ones vacation or golf or have a complete medical exam (too expensive for most West Virginians, many of whom can't afford health insurance) at The Greenbrier Hotel, a beautiful moneyed, rarefied, storied place in southern West Virginia situated near the sweet little town of Lewisburg, where you can treat yourself to the best apple dumplings around. The Greenbrier Valley is a picturesque, relatively flat valley that is uncommon in West Virginia and is a developer's dream. Farmers there, like everywhere else, are selling off. Farmers in West Virginia have historically fought losing battles against business interests.

The Greenbrier is a place for Congressional retreats, but a place where many West Virginians may be, as my mother was, a little uncomfortable—being suspicious of afternoon tea timers. Someone once said to me with more than a bit of amazement, "The Greenbrier is in West Virginia?" This perhaps was excusable but the person asking me this had actually stayed at The Greenbrier. I've heard the complaint from a few comfortable if not well-heeled West Virginians who have been to the Greenbrier Hotel on business, when the pleasure is at least tax deductible, that the "service is not what it used to be." The Greenbrier is still a five star oasis of luxury if you can afford it. It was the place where, during WWII, German and Japanese ambassadors were housed—it is hard to term The Greenbrier a prison or detention center. The Greenbrier also had a huge underground bunker—now a tourist attraction—for the Congress and the President and his entourage in case of foreign attack. I guess the powers that be decided that if our own citizens couldn't find West Virginia, no foreign enemy could. That is still perhaps a partial reasoning behind the secret government complex in the eastern mountains of West Virginia. It is somewhat ironic that a place supposedly as mysterious and remote as West Virginia should be so close to our nation's capital.

Mountaineers are rooted in the land, in each other and in their state pride. Lack of good roads and transportation may have made people more dependent on each other and family bonds tighter. Today, two-thirds of West Virginians still live in towns with a population of 3,000 or less. Only a third of West Virginia could be classified as remotely urban. Charleston, the state capital, has only 55,000 people. There are a couple of areas that are city size and a half-dozen communities that are town size. The rest vary in size from a 100 or so to 2,000 or 3,000 in places that usually sit cozily between a couple of mountains. I like saving driving time on the interstates, but I miss all the little towns along the way on the hilly, narrow, curvy roads—except for those times when stuck behind a coal truck.

Mountaineers aspire for simplicity. Ironically while many Afghans have no formal education, and no "things," they may be more aware of what the things they have are made of. The Afghans know where their bread comes from, what their bed is made out of. We see how hard life is there and appreciate what we have and the freedom that has allowed individuals to be inventive and productive, while building a complex country. Yet we yearn for simplicity. Complexity makes our lives easier on one hand and more stressful on the other. Grandma Dessie, my dad's mother, lived the simple life that Thoreau preached. Her back was bent from years of work as a house cleaner, one of the few jobs available to women at that time. After Grandpap died, she moved into town and I can still see her going up the darkened stairs to her two-room apartment carrying a bag of groceries, using the

My Grandmother Dessie.

handrail to pull her eighty-something-year-old-body up the long flight of steps. But lighting up each dark step was her beautiful smiling face. She had a twin sister named Bessie. As a child I always thought the names funny, and they still bring a smile, like the women always did who bore the names.

Dessie and Bessie were women of the mountains, like my mother's mother, Elizabeth. They were strong, tough, unsentimental women, yet gracefully soft with a sense of humor that belied the rigors of their lives. They were irreplaceable as is the loss of wilderness from which they came. We could learn a thing or two from our ancestors about living, about responsibility. They knew where their dinner came from. Nothing was thrown away. There was a use for most everything. There are so many modern conveniences now that didn't exist then, but there were lessons to take that perhaps we have forgotten. We don't know how to make candles or save seeds from year to year or how to make soap or dye or how to set a broken bone. Not that we need to or possibly can know how everything that affects our lives is put together, but it seems we could stand to be a little more rounded and not so dependent.

One could ask who wants to go back and live the lives of our ancestors? I hypothesize that many would prefer the peaceful, bucolic mountains of yesteryear to the explosion of demand for coal that has made many lives hell. Now we think we don't need to know how anything works, including state government. But not knowing keeps us out of the loop on matters that are vital to our survival. I, like most, have gladly consumed and taken for granted the electricity that coal produces through the efforts of people like my relatives and forbears.

My father's life on the farm was hard but relatively serene and safe. Two World Wars, the Depression, and the Korean War had little effect on life on the farm, leaving it much the same as when Lincoln had granted West Virginia statehood, when you could settle on land for two cents an acre. In fact there hadn't been much change in the last 300 years as far as farm life went. The farm had carried my Dad's family through the Depression, when many others were struggling.

During the winter of 1933 there were tent cities in West Virginia. The farm still provided for us when I was a boy. We had moved to the farm out of a basement apartment we had lived in briefly after Dad returned from the war. The move was a transitional period while Dad was building a house in town.

Those days on the farm were a child's delight, though there was no gas, electricity or running water. There was no radio or television. All the fireplaces and the kitchen stove used coal. There was a fireplace in every room, the only source of heat, but mostly only the kitchen and sitting room had a fire going. Whenever you needed some coal, you got your pick and shovel, walked to the family coal mine, and chipped away. The coal was shoveled into a small bin on tracks and then the bin was rolled back to the mine entrance where the coal was shoveled again from the bin to the truck. Grandpap would take me along, and I would get to carry my own small pail of coal back to the house.

There was a well for water 180 feet down. By the time you got the water up, you needed a drink—the best tasting water I ever drank. When I got a little older, it was one of my jobs to wind up the rope attached to the long cylinder tin dispenser and unload that pure fresh spring water. There was a cistern off the side of the house to collect rainwater for washing clothes and dishes and bathing. I was afraid of the dark, deep cistern even though it had a wooden slat cover on it. I had dreamed that there were snakes swimming in the bottom. You would put your pail on a hook at the end of a pole and lower the bucket down into the dark water. Grandma would heat the water on the stove for bathing. Everybody bathed one by one in a galvanized tub in the kitchen.

There were blocks of ice to keep perishables. The light from kerosene lanterns lit the evenings with a soft glow. It was nice and cozy—made cozier by the voice of Bing Crosby on the wind-up phonograph. Of course about twenty yards from the house, there was an outhouse with the proverbial Sears, Roebuck catalogue. There had been no attempt to dress up the outhouse architecturally. It was simply practical and smelly. There was a chamber pot in the bedrooms for use at night. I slept on a feather tic mattress that Grandma made. It practically swallowed me. It was wonderful, a great luxury. When I slept with Grandpap, it was in the nude. He'd say, "Best way to sleep, boy." Grandma quilted all the quilts on all the beds. Most of those beds had been handmade by my great-grandfather. There were cars, vintage 1930. I recall after the war, Dad letting me steer the car one time, down Grand Street in Morgantown with me in his lap. The brakes failed, and we smashed into a funeral procession.

The horse was still depended on to pull the plow. When I got strong enough, Grandpap let me hold the plow and make the planting rows straight. Grandma put her heavy black irons on the stove to heat them up so she could iron. She made her dresses from the many colorful feed sacks that she bought at the feed store down on the river. There were all sorts of fruit trees, cherry, apple, peach, pear, plum, walnut trees, and hickory trees along with maple, oak, locust, ash, and elm. We would collect nuts, keeping the walnuts in their green coat on paper in the basement to let them dry out. Then we would remove the outer layers and the dark stain would cover our hands and finally we would crack the hard shells and remove the fruit so that Mom could make fruitcakes and nut rolls. My favorite was blackberry picking. It was a delight when I came upon a bush loaded with berries. I still love blackberry, peach, and strawberry jams—I had my own strawberry patch.

The land was craggy with rocks and hilly, difficult farmland; but it provided shelter, food, water, and enough flat areas for planting. It was land that motivated my ancestors crossing the mountains, land where battles were fought, land that provided fuel for heat and cooking, land that provided trees for building furniture and houses. It was land that had provided all the necessities for every member of many generations, but also land where mineral rights were sold. Dad didn't know this until he and his brother decided a good many years ago to see if they could make a few extra dollars by strip mining for coal. They were surprised when paid a visit by a man who said he owned all the mineral rights under their ground. All hopes for some extra money were shot down, and Dad and his brother joined a long list of West Virginians who didn't own what they thought they did.

The garden grew everything we needed: potatoes, tomatoes, corn, cucumbers, onions, pole beans, carrots, lettuce, and radishes. There were hogs to butcher. I made the rounds with Grandpap to slop the hogs and feed the chickens. I would collect the eggs. I don't recall Grandpap going hunting, though he must have or knew someone who did because there was the occasional squirrel and rabbit meat along with deer meat at the dinner table. You didn't have to be much of a hunter in those days. Just open the door, and dinner was liable to be in the yard.

Grandpap didn't have any cows, but his daughter, my Aunt Elsie, and my Uncle Burn were dairy farmers. Their farm bordered Grandpap's. It was there I learned how to milk cows. They had a helper, Charley. In all those years, I never heard Charley speak more than twenty words. He was shy as a mouse, but had a wonderful smile warmed by the kindest soul. Grandpap had given Burn and Elsie some land, which was a bone of contention with my dad and his brother, especially after Burn and Elsie sold off all the trees to a logger, leaving the land as bare and cold as an iceberg.

Every Sunday morning, Grandpap would take his axe, and pinning a chicken on a dark, bloodstained tree stump, he would chop off the chicken's head. I would close my eyes as the headless chicken careened around the dead stump. Later, I would watch Grandma pluck the feathers and then scrub the bald chicken before dropping it into a big pot on the coal-fired stove. I dreaded eating supper and convinced myself that the Sunday ritual of beheading a chicken was a partial reason why I became a vegetarian.

After supper, we would make ice cream, but it seemed to take a lot of work and time. For an impatient child, I couldn't understand all the bother. It was easier to buy a cone of ice cream in town at Chico's Dairy that tasted much better to me.

There was a porch where, weather permitting, everyone sat after dinner or all day on Sundays. Grandpap, without ever moving out of his rocker, was an expert fly swatter. The adults would make sporadic conversation, and even that wasn't easy because there wasn't a real talker in the bunch, but they were as solid as the porch they sat on. The children would listen to the sparse talk about neighbors and kin and watch the deer appear on the hill over the shed and eventually all were quiet as the solitude of evening fell. It was the routine of rural life that had been playing out for generations.

My ancestors had no gift for accumulation. Many things on the farm from my childhood, like kerosene lamps, milk cans, tools, were mostly sold or given away. There were antiques perhaps, but for some it was just "old stuff laying around." So there are no objects with the dust of my ancestors, no hat racks or hats or canes. The farm was never really much of a gathering place for past or present relatives. It was not a summer place, no retreat, no nostalgia allowed. Life did not permit the indulgence. My ancestors have been on the farmland for 200-plus years, and yet there is no great sense of ritual aside from the Sunday dinner. There seemed to be no stories passed down of the kind that bind generations together. There was and is a love that has been pure through the generations of kin, but there has been no fabled Dylan Thomas aunt and uncle stories.

Mountaineers have always had a strong inclination to assert their autonomy. We don't like anyone telling us what to do. This

My Grandma McIntyre.

prideful independence is good as long as we don't let it get in our way. It took some time to get a seat belt law on the books and seven years to get a helmet law passed for children motor bikers. Mountaineers like my father, like many West Virginians, never wasted time on trying to be what they weren't. Mountaineers by nature, by upbringing, are loners. They are firm believers in discipline. They don't like abortion and think more folks should go to church. They are partial to guns (61% are gun owners) and morality.

One mountain trait is that hill people don't like to make a big fuss about things. They won't turn in their neighbor for running moonshine. Not wishing to cause trouble is one of the traits the coal companies and others have used to their advantage. Still West Virginians don't feel particularly victimized. They know there are no rights; the vessel is empty, waiting to be filled, waiting, as in Hayden's Creation, for order out of chaos. What is West Virginia's destiny? Will enough of it still be intact for some future leaders to fulfill the promise that many saw for its future? Why should we care? Rachel Carson writes, "Underlying the beauty of the spectacle there is meaning and significance. It is the elusiveness of that meaning that haunts us, that sends us again and again into the natural world where the key to the riddle is hidden."[4] I have always felt that West Virginia was the key to my riddle.

Saturday night, if not what it used to be when the miners cashed their paychecks and went to town to raise a glass or two, is still a time to let your hair down. Mountaineers do poke fun at themselves among themselves. It is their comment on the perception that some hold of mountain people. They are so used to hearing and reading disparaging and discouraging things about the state that they have developed a gallows humor. "We ain't dumb, we jist don't know no better." "I gotta git up and git my food stamps." Individuality has always been important to West Virginians, to all Americans. It is our heritage. "You are as good as the next man" has been ingrained in lore if not in fact. There is truth that West Virginians are distinctive, and that is good. Arthur Schlesinger, Jr., wrote:

> *How can masculinity, femininity, or anything else survive in a homogenized society, which seeks steadily and benignly to eradicate all differences between the individuals who compose it? If we want to have men again in our theatres and our films and our novels, not to speak of in our classrooms, our business offices, and our homes, we must first have a society which encourages each of its members to have a distinct identity.*[5]

The value of each individual in God's sight is ultimate and absolute. We know, cloning and identical twins aside, that modern DNA has taught us that each human being alive today differs genetically from any other human being and is probably different from any other human being that has ever lived. West Virginians need to take time to look at each other with renewed appreciation, respect, and love. We need to remind ourselves that each one of us has a distinct identity. Each one of us is important for the survival of the whole. To realize that your life has value is a blessing. You feel restored. To find that you are accepted and appreciated is to be found and to be given a home.

Friendliness permeates the mountain air, floating like a warm breeze over the state. Mountaineers are polite. My mother was always instructing me to be polite, to say thank you. There is among the people of West Virginia a great fortitude and a strong sense of loyalty. This kinship goes back to the earliest times when folks were self-supporting and really were dependent on each other. If a mountain community has a problem, a disaster of sorts, West Virginians drop whatever they are doing and pull together like no others. They have had a lot of practice.

When our country is at war, West Virginians serve in numbers like no others—West Virginia has the 4th highest per capita population of military volunteers in the nation. It is home to 184,000 vets. One county, McDowell, has the highest percentage of enlisted men in the country.[6] This is probably due more to a dearth of choices at times than patriotism. I thank my father and other veterans for their service—for without it, I might not be here. Mountaineers unwaveringly support the troops. Veterans like my dad and other West Virginians mute any criticism of the war in Iraq, but they are voicing complaints among themselves, and as Dad said, "What a mess."

Mountaineers like my father didn't and still don't have a lot of patience for those who don't buy "made in the USA." There were not many low priced Japanese cars back in the 1980s on West Virginia roads, and though Pearl Harbor was long behind us, it was still fresh in a lot of minds around those parts. Like many, Dad hasn't forgotten the bombing of the *West Virginian* at Pearl Harbor. However, the climate warmed somewhat when Toyota announced that it would build a car plant in West Virginia. This was like hitting the lottery. The plant to this day is successful and the West Virginia workers productive.

My Dad had always voiced skepticism, or maybe the fitter term is outright hostility, about anything foreign. He has never touched Japanese food, but now brags on the 1996 Toyota he bought. It has 14,000 miles on it and was actually bought by Mom. Dad had told her to go buy a car that she liked and she did. He had no idea it was a Japanese car when Mom bought it. "Like brand new," he beamed with pride about the Toyota as we drove around town. "It's Japanese," I smilingly reminded him. "Those people can make cars. Your mother liked it. She said the car we had was too big," (an Oldsmobile, a car that Dad finds hard to believe is no longer built). "She didn't like to drive it." Suddenly, fuming with frustration he said, "Why can't we build cars like this? Tell me that, will you?" We pulled into the parking lot of Bob Evans, Dad's favorite restaurant. He struggled to get out of his seat belt. "Why can't those Japanese design better seat belts?"

Mountaineers are fairly closed-mouthed, except when it is felt one of them does something good in the world; then there is a welcoming that is as pleasing and heartfelt as one has ever had. They always have kind words for those who did not forget where they came from, just as they might condemn and judge a person they suspect of being cowardly or "snooty" or "wishy-washy" and will bring the roof down on anyone morally corrupt or on a lawyer who "thinks he's better than anyone else." Jerry West, the great Hall of Fame basketball player for the Lakers, is a West Virginia hero, as is Sam Huff, the great football player who went on to play for the New York Giants. They are West Virginians who played their respective sports first at West Virginia University.

They continue to be two of the most recognized faces in West Virginia. It is hard to translate how popular they are, how much they are looked up to. They are held with pride by the people of West Virginia and showered with adulation. Here are two true "Mountaineers," both born into the hard humble living conditions of coal mining communities, who could play with the best in the world. West and Huff carried an entire state's hopes and dreams with them. West Virginians followed every game that West and Huff played. Upon returning to West Virginia, they were greeted with the enthusiasm reserved for conquering heroes.

"I Like Ike" pins were handed out in my grade school. Adults wore them in their lapels. Ike's face was everywhere in the early fifties; but even as President he could not compete with Huff and West. John Kennedy, who kicked off his cash-dispensing presidential campaign in West Virginia in 1960—a campaign that benefited Kennedy far more than West Virginia—could not compete with West and Huff in the hearts of West Virginians. Huff and

West were served up as inspirations, examples of West Virginians who had "done good." Chuck Yeager, the famous test pilot, and Pearl Buck, the writer, were also inspirations, along with numerous others, but perhaps not on the level of our two most celebrated sportsmen. It had a great deal to do with knowing that our own had gone out into the world and competed with the best and had come out victorious.

West Virginians want to be self-sufficient. They do not like to say they need help. But many in the state need help because of the lack of economic opportunities. Helping sort out Dad's finances, I was confronted with the depth of his distrust and resentment, especially when it came to money. Mom had always paid the bills. There was a perhaps deserved suspicion of anything that he did not understand, and he wanted to know why I needed to know. "It's my money. I'll do with it as I want." Mountaineers hold onto their pride and independence and their past.

Dad now talks readily of the past, perhaps because that is all he feels he has ahead. If a way of life has been fulfilling, there is no reason to change it. Mountaineers carry their baggage of prejudices, social and political, and some are unable or unwilling or don't see the need to change old habits. At times a lack of information and knowledge about the world feeds the darker aspects of our being. This unknowing, being uninformed, afflicts us all.

There is in me an affinity with the extended family of West Virginians. I was and am one of them not only by birth but also by inheritance and conviction. I have felt a sense of security and, until recent years, a certainty in West Virginia. It will always be a familiar and sacred place to live. I share with other "mountaineers" a desire for an uncomplicated life.

Something tells me that moving to a simpler life will take a long time. We will have to readjust our comfort level as to what an uncomplicated life means in terms of today's world.

5

"COUNTRY ROADS"

The late John Denver's song "Country Roads," with the words "Mountain mama, West Virginia, take me home…country roads…almost heaven, West Virginia" became a hit in the early 1970s. The fever with which people took to the song inspired the tourism department to try and capitalize on the song's popularity. The song is revered and at this writing plays on a commercial, extolling "positive" images of West Virginia. I don't know that Denver had ever been to West Virginia before the song's debut, but after he sang the song at the halftime of a university football game and the crowd sang joyously in unison with him, you knew things could not be better.

As football goes, the state goes. On several Saturdays every fall, enough fans from around the state head to Morgantown, home of West Virginia University, to make it for a few hours the largest city in the state, and they all join in the state's largest sing-a-long of "Country Roads." Denver was adopted as a prized citizen, and the song soon became an anthem for the state. It was our "Star-Spangled Banner."

When the song first hit the charts, West Virginians wherever were calling each other; "Have you heard the song? It's about West Virginia." People were ecstatic. West Virginia had never had that kind of widespread positive exposure in a song. There are not very many West Virginians who can't sing at least a bar or two of "Country Roads." I bought two copies and know all the words. As I sat in my St. Louis hotel room in December of 2004 revising this chapter, it seemed an omen that an old John Denver concert was playing on the local PBS station; and I swear that when I tuned it in, Denver was singing "Country Roads." The people clapped and sang along. The song romanticizes my home state, and the song's simplicity works; it tugs at my heart and makes me a little homesick.

On an elevator in Montreal years ago, "Country Roads" was playing and I could not resist singing along. I smilingly explained to the two other passengers—American I might add—that I was from West Virginia! "Where is it?" I had no retort. I just continued to sing along with John and glorify in "Country Roads," a place that once was as good as the song made it sound. Or was it? Had that place ever existed? If it did, had it vanished not long after the first coal seam was discovered?

Denver's "Country Roads" is not meant to deal with the complexities of life. The song, like the state, is not complicated—they just reside in a complicated world. The song is like the simple grace of a picket fence. A picket fence, like West Virginia, means comfort, inviting, cozy, nice folks, gentle, homey. You know an apple pie is baking in the oven of a house behind a picket fence. The smell of freshly baked bread tells you that there is real life happening there. It is a wish for security and warmth. It is making order out of chaos.

A picket fence does what John Denver's song "Country Roads" does; it draws you in, like a good painting. You know someone is at home that cares and you forget acquisitions and consumption. Behind a picket fence lives someone you can trust, who knows the value of a good rocker with wide arms and a high back, who has a blackberry cobbler cooling on the windowsill. Or is all this just plain old nostalgia or wishful thinking? Have I been in Hollywood too long? Is "Country Roads" just another way to hustle authenticity? Perhaps the picket fence is the myth that some of us search or wish for. Perhaps it only means, "Keep out," and just look nicer than land mines or barbed wire on top of chain link fences.

 The song confirms for us and tells the rest of the country that West Virginia is as quaint as a rocking chair—albeit where the unemployed and underemployed can sit and rock away their worries. They can have another beer, lose another job, take another drug, light another cigarette, have another helping of biscuits and gravy, and watch some more television while listening to "Country Roads" and looking for someone to fall in love with. The song is probably responsible for some people returning to their roots, back "to the place where I belong," where "life is older than the trees and younger than the mountains."

A friend was recently on a holiday cruise for a week and kept hearing "over and over this song about West Virginia." I sang a few bars of "Country Roads" for her, and she said, "That's it!" She had been cruising with 110 enthusiastic West Virginians. The song was a warm fuzzy for the state and its people and ironically reminds people of a quaint past that some of them want to forget. Maybe that is the song's allure. "Country roads, take me home…" to a simpler time, where there were no responsibilities.

It was and is hard to escape the need to embrace the charm of the song. It continues today to puff us up, uplift us, give us a renewed sense of pride that allows people to look and feel beyond the demeaning image of the ignorant hillbilly. When the song hit the airwaves, it took our minds off our problems.

Another state hero is Senator Robert Byrd. If we were lucky, Senator Byrd would get money for a prison for McDowell County and every other county while he was at it. Thirty odd years later, there is still hope for more prisons, more detention centers for the young. At the rate people are going to jail for mandatory sentencing for drug possession in West Virginia, the prisons will be needed. West Virginia spends 3.7% more per prisoner than per public school pupil.[7]

Today we still look to "Country Roads" to feel good. The song's words "Almost heaven," despite the "dark and dusty painted on the sky," still speaks to the heart and sentimentality of many West Virginians, although much of southern West Virginia still suffers from high poverty and few job possibilities. The reaction to John Denver's song was and is somewhat akin to a man in the desert finding water or a drowning man being tossed a life preserver. West Virginians starving for attention grasped a straw in the wind because that's mostly what they get from a thing called progress. The coal companies must love Denver's song because it makes West Virginians feel good.

In the fall of 2003, West Virginia University's football team gave a "whupping" to the number three-ranked team in the country, giving the state a temporary high—jubilation reigned. Many fans wanted to hear and sing the song "Country Roads" after winning. Singing the song had become a tradition. University officials said that the plan was for the band to play "Country Roads" and the students would sing along, but there was a snafu in communications.

Students on this particular day rushed to the playing field to celebrate with the team and sing "Country Roads," but the song wasn't played, so one assumes that's why the students rioted. Rampages were going on outside the stadium, fires were being set, rocks, and bottles were thrown. The police resorted to using pepper spray to quell the joyous students trying to tear down the goalposts. Another estimated 5,000 students had to be dispersed from jubilant celebrating.

The *Los Angeles Times*, furthering the stereotyping of West Virginia, reported, "garbage and couches had been removed from porches four days prior to the game in an attempt to prevent bonfires." This meant that rioting was expected. Was this a tired image reinforced once again, confirming what the nation already thought?

Just recently, I received some calls about an article in the *New York Post* reporting that West Virginia University was in the top ten schools nationwide for marijuana use, consuming hard liquor, and good old partying. One New Jersey friend said that West Virginia University had become the school of choice for high school graduates in a certain New Jersey community. I assume the students made their choice of schools before the dubious newspaper article of distinction appeared, or perhaps they made their choice because of it.

Why the need to celebrate so exuberantly, with such rawness, after a football victory? Because the students didn't get to sing "Country Roads?" Was this just another indication of how violent and non-caring today's society is? These post football game celebrations are admittedly carried out on other college campuses. None are conducted in a very attractive manner, and they are all somewhat self-destructive.

There seemed to be some notion that Denver's song would maybe lull the students into a post game dream-like state where everything is wonderful, and after singing the song, the students would go home serenely happy and watch reruns of Mr. Rogers while having a hot chocolate. It seems a stretch to suggest that the students were so disappointed at not getting to sing "Country Roads" that they rioted.

Could there be other reasons for the rioting besides just poor behavior by a bunch of students? I think being from West Virginia, the perception (perception being reality) of West Virginia, infects its people whether they are natives or not. People contract these infectious feelings just below the surface, feelings that are ready to burst out saying, "West Virginia is something to be reckoned with."

That is somewhat the feeling I had when as a young actor, I portrayed Reverend Gordon Batelle in the 1961 premiere production of the outdoor drama *Honey In The Rock*. It is a play set in the Civil War and performed every summer night at Grandview Park's 1,400-seat amphitheater in Beckley. The play centers on the founding of West Virginia, in which Reverend Batelle played a significant role. That this play still runs every summer is testament to the compelling story it tells. The play's message of the honey being drained from the rock, the streams and rivers being polluted, and the forests decimated reverberates stronger today than when Kermit Hunter wrote it. His lines "You sold to the highest bidder…so he could exploit you and give nothing back" are answered with "Perhaps in a sense West Virginia has been destroying itself."

At the end of the play I spoke the line, I'm sure rather dramatically, "God bless West Virginia." It was hard to control my emotions and the tears flowed without my really knowing why. I looked forward to that moment every night because I could feel the audience's attention, and the young actor gloried in this. But it wasn't the emotion of a trained actor that was behind the tears. It was something deeper in a raw-boned young man that I did not understand. It got so that I tried not to cry. People would comment to me how moved they had been and loved the line "God bless West Virginia." My emotion had nothing to do with acting, and everything to do with how thoroughly West Virginia and the lay of that land had been ingrained in me. I believe that same emotion is somewhat evident in West Virginia's students of today.

Perhaps if the students had soberly and joyously danced and sung their way through campus wearing their gold and blue while proudly waving the West Virginia flag, the reporting would have taken on a positive tone.

West Virginia has a proud history, but we cannot deny or dismiss the underlying reasons for the raw emotion. We have let the state's public image be largely decided by outsiders, just as today America seems to be letting the terrorists win the propaganda war for America's world image. This seems to me to be a suitable subject for a college course at the University.

West Virginians certainly need to have other and perhaps better reasons to celebrate than a football victory—which was portrayed as "the greatest win in West Virginia's history." The subsequent celebration far surpassed that year's celebration of West Virginia's 140th year of statehood. The need to jump up and down and throw arms and everything else in the air that glorious fall day even reached southern California as I jumped for joy on hearing the final score, much as I did after the string of West Virginia victories in the 2005 NCAA basketball tournament.

One of the players commented after one basketball victory, "I hope they don't burn the town down." Can a battle after victory be blamed, as I read after the noted football victory, on a few lunatics, several drunks and cokeheads? Was the celebration just some good fun? Can a winning football team rally a state in need of rallying? Indeed it can.

West Virginians need things to shout about, or at least there is the perception that they need things to shout about, to smile about. The historic football victory provided a bit of psychological diversion. It brought people together. Football success brings attention to the state, gives it validity. Perhaps more people will learn where the state is located. West Virginia's image is not lost on the students. What they must learn is that their image is West Virginia's image.

The nostalgia we feel is problematic. West Virginians on the whole don't welcome change, at least not a lot. It's a bit of a quandary because we like the old days, but we need to move into the 21st century. This quandary works to the advantage of the coal companies but probably to the disadvantage of the young. West

My father and Grandmother Dessie on the farm in 1981.

Virginians relish doing things and repeating things that past generations have done. We sort of like to think that the state has been exempt from the push of time, like the old family retreat on some remote island. At least that is what we tell ourselves. This has been the wish, the desire of many "mountaineers." But basically mountaineers are just tired of watching a small number of people getting rich at their expense.

Today's hill children are leaving their "country roads" and heritage in record numbers. Many young people today have no choice but to leave. West Virginia is unable, some say because of its regressive tax structure, to support its family. The working people who stay face financial burdens. West Virginia has one of the oldest populations in the country—an average of 38.1 years of age.

The population has leveled out the last couple of years, but the birth rate is very low because of the exodus of the young.

Mountaineers today have to search to find the contented idyllic life of "Country Roads" that my cousins Bill and Carolyn Sabo found as children in the town of Petersburg, where the South Branch River was flush with fish and the woods full of wild turkey. This is the mountain background and heritage we dream of, we have images of, the "Wild, Wonderful, West Virginia," independence. How will my father's youthful club motto, "all for one and one for all," fare in the ever-increasing technology, education, and income gap of today? It has not fared too well for many mountaineers, proud as they are of West Virginia; they may wonder if they have been served up a false promise of independence; but still we all want to buy into it. We have been sold and have convinced ourselves of the proud myth that "Mountaineers are always free."

Most who leave entertain going back to West Virginia after they reach retirement age because the state is still remote enough that you really can be laid back and enjoy a hike and a river view that doesn't empty your wallet. Individuality and serenity are often stated by mountain folks as why they stay in West Virginia or in some cases why they have moved there. The things they say that draw them to West Virginia, where kin folk of generations back are drawn like a magnet, like a moth to light, include words like pride, independence, tradition, freedom, family, frontier, breath-taking unspoiled mountain beauty, the kind my Dad described as "sky-blue beauty that hurts the eyes." These words, as Lincoln might say, "don't scour." But for West Virginians, the words still ring true because they want to believe them, even though some West Virginians say they are more pessimistic today than yesterday and don't see much potential for the state. But mountaineers are stubborn, and independence is still held as something sacredly ordained when in fact it was compromised long ago, like the wilderness. Mountaineer independence is on its deathbed. A ceremony is being prepared to pay tribute to what was stolen away, to what could have been.

This clinging to individuality in West Virginia seemingly has no limits, no obligations. This independence of "don't tell me what I can or can't do," or "I don't want any cares," has had a steep price. Basic rights have been trampled. The idea that one can live cheaply, out of the rat race, in the beautiful mystical Appalachians where God put enough land for all of us, where folks can hunt and fish to their heart's content, where everyone minds his own business is a fool's paradise today. What happened to those fundamentals that guided some—those who weren't looking out for their own interests—who fought for the right for West Virginia to break away from Virginia? Some of the young see in West Virginia a kind of angry resignation—what will be will be—there is nothing to be done—this is West Virginia, what can you possibly hope for. Everything—once West Virginia gets the big boot of economic exploitation off its neck.

There is a seemingly unending parade of negativity that can best be described as mountain fatalism, a fatalism that is encouraged, breeds, is highly contagious, and is passed down from generation to generation, and one has to treat it with all the care one would any serious disease. My mother's father said to my dad about the perilous conditions of the mine, "Ain't a dang gum thing you can do about it." We all took his words to heart—none of us went into the mines.

Grandpap McIntyre just had to go on with a "when it's my time" attitude, "what will be will be." He was a crippled and broke life-long coal miner with the barest of possessions and died not long after uttering those words—thinking (brainwashed) that his suffering was necessary. He kept his humor, sharp mind, pride, grace and love for his grandchildren till the end. He wanted to be able to give us something tangible. He did. He gave us the strength and fortitude to go forward.

Like the Native Americans who were not considered human and who were exploited, stripped of their lands and placed on reservations, West Virginians have suffered a systematic destruction. The state in the past was never really thought of by outsiders as a place to be seen and experienced but rather one to be exploited and endured. Today there is a growing tourist trade, but that could be jeopardized by the "rape and take" greed of certain coal companies. Mining and logging are two of the pillars on which this country was built. So many lives have been torn apart, disrupted simply because of greed, by using workers and then letting them fall aside when they are used up.

In the southern counties, where even the state's governors don't like to visit without a deployment of state troopers, the people have turned to drugs and other life-destroying habits. The powerful painkiller OxyContin, dubbed "Hillbilly heroin," has been and is a problem in every county.[8] Some dealers are older, disabled seniors. What happened to good old moonshine? Pot is the crop of choice. Cocaine is widely available, Methamphetamine use is surging; it is a large threat in Wood County and elsewhere. The West Virginia young, according to statistics, are desperately trying to get out, trying to survive. The proud, independent, and truly free mountaineer should be on the endangered species list.

One mountaineer who was truly proud, independent and caring was our dear friend Gus Fisher, a native of Elkins, West Virginia. He was another mountaineer who had to leave his beloved state in order to build a life. Gus lived ten minutes or so from us in Los Angeles. He never lost his love of the Mountain State and would call whenever he read or saw something about West Virginia. He tried to visit his home place of Elkins at least once a year. Gus passed away in February of 2004. His daughter said that he would have wanted "Country Roads" played at his funeral. So my wife and I sat and listened to John Denver sing his infectious song once more, and we thought of Gus and West Virginia, and we cried. The tears were at once joyful and grateful for the friendship of an inspiring mountaineer.

6

WEST VIRGINIA MOON REVISITED

Geographic, social, and moneyed isolation have long been used to group mountain people together. But it is the blanket stereotyping of mountain people that is dehumanizing, especially when there is no attempt to liken them to the rest of the country, where there are assumedly many states of mind and ways of life. While "Mountaineers" have no desire to be like the rest of the country, they are not hick clones. They are a wide mixture of colors and ethnicity and background with a common love of their state and country. They are as varied as the patchwork quilts my grandmother made that are across my bed today; as varied as the residents of any state or country.

To exploit as well as stereotype people is to extract from them their dignity and creativity and to keep them chained to their struggles. There are many clichéd sayings to depict such behavior: keep them on the dole or down on the farm, or the barrio, or ghetto, or up in the coal camp barefoot, tired, poor, and miserable—and the women pregnant—or by keeping them lined up along the streets begging for work. Damaging or stealing their identity has been performed as cleanly as the extraction of the natural wealth of the hills, as precisely and efficiently as the surgeon's extraction work on my grandmother's clotted veins.

Supposedly the first film made in West Virginia was *Tol'able David* in 1921. It depicted mountaineers as barefoot, shotgun toting, menacing, dangerous criminals. Excepting West Virginians, nobody seems to put a good take on a place where the latest trendy fashion may blessedly arrive a few months late. Starbucks just came to the state and one writer noted: "It means the state can change the motto on their license plates to: West Virginia. Fewer Starbucks than front teeth."

Michael Ramirez, the political cartoonist, drew a cartoon of two Appalachians on the porch of their shack—along with an old tire and sleeping pig, hanging underwear, kerosene lamp, and "moonshine" apparatus. A woman in her feed sack dress watching television says, "Says here, any two people can be married in California." The man with a piece of straw in his mouth and holding a jug of liquor replies, "Sis, We's moving to Caleeforni-aye." The media has been responsible for spreading this oafish perception of mountain people, or as in the film *Deliverance*, of violent, vulgar, sadistic animals. Kevin Pittsnogle, the only West Virginia native on West Virginia University's 2005 basketball team, commented on stereotypes: "When I was younger, it bothered me. Not any more. I've got all my teeth. I wear shoes."

Jack Kennedy's run for the presidency turned a spotlight on West Virginia. Until then I didn't know how bad off we were. I, like others, grew tired of seeing newspaper pictures where an unforgiving lens was pointed up another hollow, or another interview ended with the result that the people had been taken advantage of or even had unintentionally been made fun of. None of these images changed a thing, but instead enforced the perception that hill people were dumb and backward, which I took subconsciously to mean—despite my education—that I must be dumb and backward—just to show how dumb and backward I was. No matter how hard some people, especially my wife, tried to combat my negative self-image, it was a losing battle. The image had become somewhat of a reality—at least in my mind.

To make matters worse, I began to apologize for my supposed shortcomings, thinking that everyone else was smarter, better educated, and more sophisticated. I used to wear the hillbilly brand like some old moth-eaten sweater. Eventually I discovered I could wear my pants with pride because I slowly began to notice that the expression "we all put our pants on the same way"—a bit of advice given to me by a wise West Virginia teacher—had some truth in it.

Despite my insecurities about myself, I have never apologized for West Virginia. I was always delighted to say whenever asked, "I'm from West Virginia." It was a real place, and a place on my return trips home as familiar as an old dream. It was where I could take friends and show them something new about their country, about myself.

Mountain folks do not often get to tell their story. My friend Earl Hamner wrote of his Appalachian upbringing in *The Waltons*. It was a family with good values and the children learned from their chores—it was character building. You believed those children would grow into adults with good heads on their shoulders. Like them, I deeply love the place I was born and raised. I was surrounded by nature's beauty and a rich heritage and was supported by caring people. Having been bitten by negative press so many times has left many West Virginians gun-shy. The press has also told us that West Virginians, if anything, are not gun-shy. "Just let em' come up here and try'n take my gun" was one recent television image.

The gun issue was a false issue in the 2004 Presidential election. It was painful to see that happen because the very real issues were ignored. Guns today in West Virginia are not just shotguns and rifles used for hunting, but include a large number of the kind of firepower familiar to most urban areas of the country today. West Virginia has a big black market in the trading of guns for drugs. There was a widely publicized sniper episode in West Virginia and once again you suspected that the news stories would reflect badly on a place "where nothing much happens." West Virginia is a place of relatively low crime—sadly the sniper story shoved it closer to the dangerous world of death and mayhem and away from the haven we want it to be.

There was a story about children who wanted to go to Broadway to be actors, but felt it was a "hopeless dream because they were from West Virginia." I understood their plight, where they were coming from, but my wife and I never felt that being from West Virginia was a road to nowhere. It would seem that talent would be the deciding factor—that and persistence and determination to prove wrong the teacher who told me to sell insurance— an honorable profession but not what I wanted to do. I once tried to set up an internship program at West Virginia University only to be told by a white male professor that the students weren't qualified.

A professional acquaintance of mine taught at a camp at a

college in southern West Virginia and found that the students all felt inferior, and it was difficult to convince them otherwise. These children are the victims of a false, dreary, frustrating, and tiresome mythology, where a symbol like the Mountaineer that represents strength, courage and independence has become associated with those familiar words: inferior, backward, hopeless, and exotic. Ironically, poor, young, white West Virginians should be able to offer unique perspectives, thus qualifying them under affirmative action.

When words such as backward and inferior enter a child's consciousness and very being, how can that child be free? How can West Virginia's motto, "Mountaineers are always free," be more than an empty promise to these children? Something insidious is in the water, along with the lead and arsenic, and that is the feeling of being extraneous, of not mattering in the scheme of things, of seeing our parents and state treated as subjects.

A friend looking through a book of pictures of people from Appalachia commented how "miserable" the people looked, "too much inbreeding." He was not joking. He held the belief that "mountain people were so isolated and living in such remote circumstances, that inbreeding was both natural and expected." What my friend saw in the pictures perhaps was the skepticism of people like him, a hostility and resentment stemming from uninformed observations. In the best of photographs, when the camera seems harsh, there can be a dignity and joy, and even love. The mountain poor in their overalls, with their bad teeth and ruddy innocent faces have always been attractive subjects for photographers and news departments. The very word "Appalachia," conjures up a negative image of poverty, cultural backwardness, and desolation. It is hard for some to see anything else—such as the value system, the sense of loyalty, and the rich heritage.

A network television president in a conversation with my lawyer made derogatory comments about West Virginians while mocking their mountain accent. He didn't know that my very respected high-powered lawyer is from West Virginia. One commentator described the Iraq prisoner abuse suspects, the Abu Ghraib guards, "as recycled hillbillies," as if where they came from (at least one was from West Virginia) explained their behavior. A health guru, on a recent PBS fundraiser, said he was from West Virginia and then proceeded to exaggerate the accent and mime his West Virginia brother's potbelly. The mountain accent is often mocked, and it's one more thing that tends to stereotype people to the point that the stereotype becomes true. We need to tell the children to be proud of their accent. My own drawl wasn't that bad, it didn't extend forever, and I couldn't detect any nasal quality but I was self-conscious. I don't say "git" for "get" anymore, but I still say "boddle" for "bottle." West Virginia still comfortably hangs on me like a favorite old sweater.

West Virginians are apt to say to any young "mountaineer" venturing out into the world, "Make us look good. Don't act like a hick from the sticks." It is a burden you carry. Not long ago, I received a call from a young West Virginia man whose band had been selected to appear in concert at a venue in Los Angeles for the top ten unsigned bands in the country. He was with good reason quite excited about his forthcoming adventure and couldn't help expressing delight for "us West Virginian boys." There's the future, the possibility. But did I detect a tinge of pessimism in his voice? Or like a lot of West Virginians was he just a hard-core realist?

It takes a certain kind of positive soul to live in West Virginia. Trials and tribulations are part of the "Surviving West Virginia" story. There is a pride and independence in facing life as it is given, good traits to have if you are of the hills. While there is courage in dealing with the realities of hill life, there is also within each the collective dream of better days ahead.

When a West Virginian does make good in the world, like basketball player Jerry West, we are proud that a West Virginian has succeeded on the world stage. Knowing that one of us has "made it," helps us all survive. I doubt that Mr. West was fond of the label "Zeke from Cabin Creek." We can look at Mr. West and hold our heads up and thumb our noses at any stereotypical notions about a richly complicated people with a past full of tragedy and history. Somehow we forget about our history. It seems some sort of an aberration. We need to grasp and hold our history, protect it, listen to those voices that fought and died for it. We need to study the past so that we don't make the same mistakes again, mistakes that have put the mountain state's future in jeopardy. We must be ready when the next exploiter comes along.

Not long ago the University of Virginia pep band lampooned West Virginia's rural hillbilly image. They depicted a *Bachelor* television episode where he chooses between two girls, one from West Virginia and one from Virginia. The girl from West Virginia was dressed as a mountain girl in denim with pigtails. West Virginia's then governor complained that the image was a stereotype that mountain people were trying to live down, and he wanted an apology. It's another diversion from the real problems. Another complaint by the Governor, while well intended, of the recent Abercrombie and Fitch T-shirts emblazoned "It's all relative in West Virginia" seemed to only pour gasoline on the fire and in the end make more money for Abercrombie. Their executives must have high-fived each other upon hearing the Governor's complaint. It would have been better for the Governor to have sported a t-shirt of his own poking fun at Abercrombie.

The stereotypical hillbilly is alive and thriving. It is this image that can be a roadblock to improving the state's economy. This is what former Governor Wise knew and why he got upset at any attempt to perpetuate a negative image. So I understand and appreciated his concern and effort to curtail such ventures. But education of the state's children and not a governor's complaint will turn the tide. Knowledge is power and cannot be taken away from you. The word hillbilly—like nigger—took on connotations such as trash and the dirt on your shoe, illiterate, something to be made fun of. James Comstock named his newspaper *The West Virginia Hillbilly,* "the newspaper for West Virginians who can't read by an editor that can't write." Comstock noted; "At the outset I didn't really understand that West Virginians didn't like to be called hillbillies."

My high school art teacher was practically tarred and feathered for a painting—*West Virginia Moon*—that reminded some of an outhouse. The painting was said to emphasize the popular image of West Virginia as a degenerate place. Joe Moss was a native West Virginian, and was my encouraging high school art teacher who told me, "Selby, you do good work, just not enough of it." Moss's painting caused convulsions and revulsions in West Virginia when

A BETTER PLACE

Joe Moss's West Virginia Moon. *Courtesy Charleston Newspapers.*

it was unveiled in the 60s. People were furious, and the sitting governor criticized it. Some said it was a slap in the face to West Virginia. Moss was branded *persona non grata* for his painting. He was labeled a communist and a destroyer of democracy.[9]

The painting was banned from being displayed after attracting the largest crowds ever for an art exhibition in West Virginia. Some years later it again was brought out for public viewing at the Huntington Museum, but once again the protests started up and the painting was put back in mothballs, never to my knowledge to be seen again in West Virginia. And what did Moss say about his painting? "West Virginia is not depressed but inactive. The figure in the doorway (referring to his painting) might be somebody unemployed or someone standing in the doorway of his home in contemplation. The framework of the old screen door represents restrictions all of us work under. The little color—oranges, yellows, reds, smoldering on the landscape—represent West Virginia's spark of potential, a flame that needs fanning."

Is banning a painting the way to defend or improve West

Virginia? If *West Virginia Moon* could create such a fuss and be banned, why can't mountaintop removal mining? Why can't two centuries of coal and timber abuse and criminal behavior? Why can't a coal company CEO's inflated salary? Why can't flagrant personal gain where public office has been used to facilitate such gain? Why can't one deplorable national ranking after another? A PAINTING!? There hasn't been a bigger commotion since the fifties, when Governor Marland tried to pass a small severance tax on coal three days into his term. Like Moss, Marland was branded a communist and run out of the state. He was later found living in Chicago driving a cab. He died shortly afterwards.

The play *The Hatfields and the McCoys,* which centers on the famous feud between the two families, plays every summer at Grandview in Beckley. Why isn't it banned? The resulting news coverage from the real event a century ago had a life of its own. The mountain people in some instances were portrayed as no more than ignorant savages. The Hatfield-McCoy feud allowed some to exploit mountain people, turning them into oafish cartoons. As Barbara Rasmussen wrote:

> In the industrial era, a petty local dispute was manipulated by absentees and their local helpers to discredit indigenous residents and exploit the resources of the area. Hatfield was forced to court so often that he had to sell the lands that outsiders coveted to pay his legal fees. Despite the colorful description of 'Devil Anse' Hatfield as a lawless, bloodthirsty, and backward mountain man, he left a long record of patient legal attempts to solve his problems. His calm rationality is a jarring contrast to the reputation that survives him.[1]

Why not bring back Moss's *West Virginia Moon* and let it draw people? Why not a book of old West Virginia outhouses? Why not sell the "real" look of a coal miner's outfit for all the folks looking for real—folks like me who buy organic and choose paper bags over plastic to carry to my American made SUV. Let a genuine hillbilly lead real experience tours throughout the state. Let people pay to see the destroyed mountains of southern West Virginia. I'm not saying stereotypes can't be damaging to the people they are aimed at; especially when we aim at ourselves. Despite the uproar over *West Virginia Moon* forty odd years ago, West Virginia is usually liberal in its views of paintings and plays. However, a book about growing up in West Virginia entitled *Crum* by Lee Maynard was banned by a store or two, ironically within a stone's throw of an annihilated mountain.

The children in Mingo and McDowell counties read *People* magazine and watch MTV. Television satellite dishes, the joke goes, are the unofficial West Virginia wildflowers. Do the children know about the good old boy politics, the bad planning, and the poor policies? Are they taught about the mountain-high debt of workers' comp? What about the depleted teachers' retirement fund? What about the rape of the natural resources? The children in Welch, West Virginia, as of this writing can't find a pay phone in town because there isn't one. They won't find a dry cleaner or laundromat either. The United States is a hard country to be poor in. Very few actually find a room at the top in this home of ours. And when some of those on top zealously, greedily, hoard their riches with no desire to take a little less so that some others can have a little more, it is frustrating and shows a clear lack of obligation to one's fellow man. We will only be touched with grace when we understand the obligation to give back. The image of America is a people rich and powerful, materialists, who have no regard for things of the mind and spirit. Yet America has depended for its very existence on the work of all sorts of great minds—even painters of such works as *"West Virginia Moon."*

West Virginian poet Muriel Dressler wrote: "I don't apologize to anyone for my background and heritage. When I hit the mountains I breathe a little sigh and say thank you Lord—I'm home."[2] Why even bring the subject up of apologizing for one's background and heritage? It may be that Ms. Dressler was just acknowledging her acquaintance and our own with the stereotypical perception of West Virginians.

7

MOUNTAINS OF COAL

It's good to maintain some mystery in this "Restoration Hardware" world. For those who discover West Virginia on their own, I'm happy for them, but I no longer carry a sandwich board around advertising the state's virtues. Oh, I still can't help myself bringing West Virginia into conversations with people—especially when told they are headed for Washington, DC and are absolutely dumbstruck how close West Virginia is. "No, not western Virginia but WEST VIRGINIA!" I then lose control and suggest points of interest that they must visit, going so far as to arrange their visits. West Virginia I assure them is a comfortable place, a place of solitude, and a place to refresh. There is a sense of grace and insulation from the outside world still found in those rolling hills that when discovered is like sunlight on a mountain hollow garden—appreciated all the more. It's just that now you may have to look a little harder and not get too nosy about what may be going on beyond the tree-lined interstates. But too many tourists aren't good for the countryside, because they will demand more and wider roads. A secret garden ought to be a little hard to find, to get to.

Once a broad plain, West Virginia through the ages was transformed with massive uplifts within the earth creating an upheaval of mountains allowing streams to cut valleys and ridges, thus exposing treasures. The plant debris over time had changed into peat. Eventually the peat through erosion compacted and slowly with heat and pressure transformed into coal. Then came the cry: "Coal! Coal!" And man would prove he really could move mountains. Fortunes would be made digging in the beloved hills but not by those doing the digging. Many Americans have made a good living thanks to the natural resources of this country. In West Virginia, coal was easy money, and easy money corrupts.

Making a living for mountaineers wasn't so easy, and conditions were not helped by the state government's not enacting a severance tax until 1967 on minerals and refusing to deal with coal refuse. Aldo Leopold wrote long ago, "We abuse land because we see it as a commodity belonging to us. When we see land as a community to which we belong, we may begin to use it with love and respect."[1] Growing up in West Virginia allowed me the pleasure of the mountains with all the serenity, beauty and surprise of Central Park in New York City. But there was more and that was the wild of a wilderness. West Virginia still has the most extensive wilderness area in the eastern United States, although true wilderness has been gone for at least a century or so, ever since Lewis and Clark started their expedition out of Harpers Ferry.

The state is a beautiful place of mountains, waterfalls, caves, grand forests and vistas. Man has infringed on that beauty. By the time I was a boy, West Virginia's wilderness had recovered from the lumber companies' early disregard for the future, but by the eighties, West Virginia again found itself under siege from coal and timber interests. The state seemed as willing as ever to ignore the adage that man and nature must live in harmony. Deforestation threatened in the nineties with its resulting problems.

In my youth when coal mining was good, the economy was better—but what about the people? A good economy didn't translate. Per capita income and employment levels were still behind national averages. West Virginia is always last or nearly so in household income. Unemployment is around 5.2%. It would be higher without the relative prosperity of the Eastern Panhandle. West Virginia is losing jobs, many to outsourcing. In Clay, Calhoun, and Mason Counties, unemployment runs from 17% to 22%. West Virginia's landfills, water-treatment plants, and sewer lines are inadequate and far worse than in surrounding states.

For as much money that has been made in coal since it was discovered in 1792, you would think that West Virginia would be another Silicon Valley before the dot.com bubble burst. There are less than two million people in the whole state, and each of them should be comfortable, but I never saw my relatives' lot improve one iota despite a lifetime digging coal. They were killed in the mines, or they coughed to death. They survived on the edge, dependent upon their feudal lords. Coal has made many people wealthy, but few of them live in West Virginia.

The most current and ruthless plundering of West Virginia is going on with mountaintop coal mining in the southern portion of the state, where one-fifth of the land has been blasted away, where 326,000 acres of Appalachian land is scheduled to be obliterated in the next seven years. Not only is mining "invasive and disruptive." In parts of southern West Virginia, it looks like the granddaddy of bombs has landed, and more bombs explode twenty-four hours a day, seven days a week, because it costs too much to stop. Three million pounds of explosives per day are used in West Virginia.[2] It is a grievous wrong overlooked for efficiency. We are left with tabletops, some of which admittedly are covered with attractive award winning tablecloths. Tabletops being the flattened mountaintops; the tablecloths being "re-forestation" efforts and reclamations.

If the mining continues unchecked, in less than two decades there will be no mountaintops left in southern West Virginia. The problems I know are many and complex for the coal industry—competition, increased regulations, judicial scrutiny. But we must look to alternative energies. Global warming is a happening that we must deal with.

Laws have been passed regulating certain coal company practices, but they are laws that some people seemingly never have any intention of obeying. Most coal fines are low even for serious violations. Coal companies are happy to pay a million dollars a month legal fee. It's a bargain to pay the fine and their lawyers. The latest statistics have West Virginia mining 148.9 million tons per year, second only to Wyoming.[3] What do the people of West Virginia have to show for this? The demand for low emission power—electricity—is enormous; coal produces more than half the electricity generated in this country and the demand is increasing. But if the goal is to enrich the lives of all people, then we must proceed beyond the immediate gratification and greed of a few. We must call forth the nation's highest morals and ethics to get the people their fair share. It is a social issue. It is a test of our nation's strength and resolve to deal with concerns such as broken families, economic security, safety—basic quality of life issues that people of West Virginia care about. Some fear that if coal mining is shut down because of higher costs for clean air and water there will be more suicides, crime, and drug addiction. Coal will not shut down. There is still a trillion dollars to be made.

The coal companies cannot see the grandeur and awe of the mountains or the human sacrifices. They are blinded not only by the dollar signs but by political pressure to deliver cheap energy. If a billion dollars can be gotten from one large mountaintop-mining project, then it begs the question, why can't a bit more of this money "trickle" down to those communities most affected? Larry Gibson, a long time opponent of mountaintop mining says that the coal industry set the value on his land at $450 million because it has thirty-nine seams of coal from one inch to twelve feet. "I'll be lucky to hold on to it."[4] How much of that money will stay in West Virginia?

Our state and federal governments have not heeded Lincoln's words where, "the substance of government, whose leading object is, to elevate the condition of men....to afford all, an unfettered start, and a fair chance, in the race of life."[5] It is people like me, too damn comfortable for our own good and too willing to enjoy my comfort at the expense of others' discomfort. We are not willing to turn out the lights.

No matter how you dress them up, the decapitated mountains can never be replaced. The graves of the mountains lie in valleys of fill—a sugarcoated phrase where "waste" was changed to "fill" in a regulation easing restrictions on the dumping. This is where the mountains are buried, where the streams have been destroyed, along with 300,000 acres of the most diverse temperate hardwood forest. According to the Environmental Protection Agency, as of 2001, more than 700 miles of streams and 400,000 acres of watershed in four states were affected by mountaintop mining removal. Hundreds of miles of streams in the coal areas have been filled in. They are gone.[6]

It is true that some of the streams are dry bed. It is also true that a coal company may clean up a mess it didn't create. The impact on wildlife has been incalculable; no matter that "wildlife awards" have been handed out for certain reclaimed sites. Many streams and rivers have been polluted with acid runoff. Fish caught in some areas are too dangerous to eat more than once or twice a month.

Not long ago high runoff from mountaintop removal mines contributed to yet another flood that devastated West Virginia. Floods cost money, lots of it, and leave little or no money to fight what causes the flooding, slack regulations. Thousands of people have seen their homes damaged or destroyed. Dangerous abandoned mine sites are less than a mile from the homes of 693,000 people in West Virginia. The Federal government has allocated 20 million dollars more to reclaim abandoned mines. That leaves 733,000 million dollars more in remaining problems.[7]

There has been a steep price to pay for the rich veins of coal in terms of the loss of lives and the destruction of the land. The southern mountains and the people need our attention and empathy, but more, they need a bigger share of the economic pie. Right now their share is but a mirage. Southern West Virginia, along with eastern Kentucky and northwest Virginia and some of Tennessee, has been sacrificed for the rest of the country's energy needs, sacrificed for the supposedly good of the country. This is not what home is about. Home is about finding ways to flourish without destroying other communities. The past and present fighters for the environment in West Virginia have not been appreciated—instead called "poverty pimps"; "do-gooders in Birkenstocks"—and have faced scorn and threats.

Some coal owners, mainly small independent ones who worked hard and faced hard times, have deserved the fruits of their labor. However, many abandoned mines operated by small companies went bankrupt so no one has the responsibility for the polluted water they discharge. The coal industry is now composed of large companies that admittedly (only because of better enforced regulations) do a better job of treating mine discharge. But on the whole, the state and federal governments still seemingly find it essential to bow to coal industry demands.[8] Yes, coal is plentiful, accessible and cheap. So raise the price and let the people in the mining areas live a decent life.

The main federal remedy has been to speed up the permitting process for mountaintop mining. A ruling in 1999 by the late, brave, and principled Federal District Judge Charles Haden said no to more dumping of rock and dirt into the hollows and streams. He wrote that such dumping was an environmental hazard and violation of the Clean Water Act. He also held that state agencies had failed to enforce laws that were in effect for mountaintop mining. President Bush was critical of Judge Haden's ruling, as were then Governor Cecil Underwood and Senator Robert C. Byrd. They said the coal industry would die in West Virginia. Judge Haden said that it was the West Virginia environment and scenery that would die. Unfortunately he lived to see his ruling overturned. The Fourth Circuit Court didn't bother with the merits of the case. The judges held that it was a state matter and that West Virginians didn't have the right to sue in federal court. No ruling has ever been made on the merits of Judge Haden's decision.

On July 8, 2004, Federal District Judge Joseph R. Goodwin issued a ruling against an Army Corps of Engineers procedure "that gives a blanket pre-clearance to Appalachian coal-mining operations." Judge Goodwin revoked eleven permits that would have created more fills and sediment ponds. The coal industry has called foul again and has appealed Goodwin's ruling.[9] I anticipate that his ruling will be overturned. "The truth is that cheap and abundant electric power is being bought at a titanic hidden and deferred cost, a cost another generation will pay with compound interest," Harry Caudill wrote in 1962 in his *Night Comes To The Cumberland's*.[10]

The land cannot be destroyed without destroying lives, without destroying one's awe of rocks and trees, of the wind that once whipped across the tops of these mountains. This is not some "poetry spouting environmental nonsense." Are we now so arrogant that we think we can use our technology to remove the very force of nature? Nature, as we are seeing, will have its revenge. Thoreau wrote, "If you would learn the secrets of nature... you must practice more humanity than others."

While the legacy that the coal companies have left is not one to be proud of, it doesn't negate the fact that coal has and continues to play a large role in West Virginia's economy and heritage. Coal reportedly puts $2.6 billion a year into the state's economy. For every dollar coal spends, supporting industries spend another five dollars.[11]

People for as long as I can remember have been scared that if coal is gone, the state will collapse. But while coal has enjoyed a dramatic upswing in its fortunes (more coal-fired power plants have been announced in the last two years than in the previous twelve years; 105 new plants are in the planning stages or under construction around the country) and is still important for the nation's economic and social well-being, change will come.[12] If we don't stand up to the fossil fuel power structure and make what will be a slow and painful transition, what are the choices? The need is to diversify away from coal and to readdress the tax structure for absentee land ownership. We also need to take back the mountains, to mine them in a responsible way. It is a delicate balance. The state is still being held captive to coal interests as another mountain goes to the highest bidder. There are 450 square miles on the planning board for strip sites.

Los Angeles buys a large part of its power from coal plants. Coal-powered power plants dumped 16 million tons of carbon dioxide, 98,000 tons of sulfur dioxide, 47,500 tons of nitrogen dioxides and 838 pounds of mercury in one year, 1999. Mercury, a by-product of burning coal, is "one of the most hazardous and ubiquitous contaminants"—one out of six babies in the U.S., 600,000 a year, is born to a mother with an elevated mercury level, which is known to interfere with brain development. Coal-fired power plants are responsible for about 48 tons of mercury released in the United States every year. The New Martinsville, West Virginia chlorine factory emitted 2,167 pounds of mercury in 2002—so there are other mercury polluters, but efforts to regulate coal power should not be any less.[13]

Burbank and Pasadena buy 75% of their power from coal plants. Coal power is 10 times cheaper than what these cities pay for solar power. Coal plants are located in places like Utah and Nevada and are fouling the surrounding air. It must be painful to live in Utah and have bad air because Los Angeles needs power for its huge electricity requirements. It's painful to live in parts of West Virginia and watch coal trucks loaded with millions in coal money go by your door when you don't even have sewage.

As the old proverb goes, "Where there is no vision, the people perish." The courts are compromised by policies that undermine environmental cases, and many feel it is a waste of time to continue fighting. People become convinced that nothing will be done. There is a mentality that says, "Oh well, there's nothing we can do, so it doesn't do any good to worry about it." The good and joyful fight goes out of people, and apathy sets in; people don't want to hear about it, it's old news. One simply doesn't care or can't care anymore because the years of abuse that the land and people have suffered under the rule of the coal companies has made people insensitive to the abuse. This abuse should bring the rafters down, but the protests seem muted considering the outrages. But fight we must because, as activist Judy Bonds says, "When these mountains go, our culture, heritage and our identity are gone. We will fight with our last breath to protect...the mountains with fierce faith."[14] Our sense of discovery falls with the mountains.

Nature is tenacious, and forests are resilient, but there is no return from a lobotomy of mountains. Some say no one will know the difference in 50 or 100 years. In a sense Annie Dillard's description of the eclipse (quoted earlier) describes the powerful catastrophic effect of mountaintop mining removal. The current Iraq war that our nation faces gives the excuse to put the plight of West Virginia and neighboring states on the back burner. There is a relationship between what is going on in Iraq and what is happening in West Virginia and Kentucky. What is going on is about oil and coal. The saddest story is what has happened to the people. Does anybody doubt that bloodshed would result if people in West Virginia armed themselves and blocked the roads, not allowing the overloaded coal trucks to leave until the companies agreed to give a fair share of the profits to the people?

Growing up in West Virginia, it was hard to not gain at least a rudimentary knowledge of coal-mining methods. Certainly I had knowledge of the way of life and death for the miners and their families. The hills of West Virginia were being raped back in the 1940s and 50s. The land was left scarred and covered with slag piles.

Harry Caudill speculated in 1962 that we were probably in the final decades of King Coal's importance as a fuel. Unfortunately this turned out to be far from true. President Bush recently stated that the United States was spending "billions on clean coal technology." The environmentalists think this is wasteful spending. If a way to burn coal cleanly is found, clean coal still isn't going to help the people. The coal companies say the people are being saved, that without them the workers would be on welfare. I guess the rest of the country buys that or just doesn't care. Besides, the notion is that the people don't know any better; that they deserve the historically bad treatment they have received for a century or so.

We have choices in our lives. The Latinos, when crossing the border, decide that the effort is worth the risk in hopes of bettering their lives. You can find a better way to mine the coal or not. You can continue to fill up the valleys and ruin the streams, or you can decide not to—a hard call for coal companies because you need someplace to dump the spoil. You can decide to share the wealth with the people or not.

The continual assault of mountaintop mining removal staggers the imagination and elevates man's greed to a new level. You wonder about the people in coal's path. George Orwell wrote, "They rise out of the earth, they sweat and starve for a few years, and then they sink back into the nameless mounds of the graveyard and nobody notices that they are gone."[15]

A popular ex-football coach at West Virginia University was hired as a pitchman for the coal industry. "I don't exactly know the regulations, but I'm smart enough to know that in China, they mine for six bucks a ton, and we have got to be able to compete with them." That will never happen. My wife and I recently returned from a tour of China, where it was hard to breathe in some areas because of the bad air caused by the burning of coal. I talked with a teacher in one of the mining areas. He told me about "black snow," and of the $150 a month wages for Chinese miners. He was witness to the deplorable and dangerous conditions under which the miners in China work; its coal industry death rate is among the world's highest—where the death toll from coal mining accidents stood at 1,113 for the first three months of 2005. Mining in America is certainly safer, but it was West Virginia that led the nation in coal mining deaths in 2004.[16]

If the "spotlight shines brighter on coal today," why is the state always behind the eight ball? Why have some miners been left without pensions? Why does the pension system for teachers have a $5 billion shortfall? (Pension liabilities exceed the state budget.) Why do budgets increase five times faster for prisons than for higher education?[17] Massey Coal Company's pension is fully funded. The company does fund and support a number of worthwhile community projects. If the coal and timber interests would take a responsible role and return a fair and just portion of the wealth they extract instead of pleading for even more tax breaks, then West Virginia's future would be a lot brighter. If West Virginia could have put the severance tax money long ago into economic development, the future would be brighter. Massey Coal can lead the way.

In this coal boom era, and despite an announced state budget surplus in June 2005, I don't know anyone who thinks the future is coming up roses for the people or the mountains of southern West Virginia. The proud West Virginians who live there don't like to read or hear stories about their place being bleak and depressed with no hope. But it is an area where most children qualify for free or reduced price federal government lunches.

Many feel the gloomy picture of the state's economic development goes back to the transfer of land and mineral rights to absentee owners. Since the turn of the last century, people have abdicated personal responsibility to the interest of coal, timber and the federal government, and thus having a pretend ownership of their state. By 1884 absentees owned one-half the land in West Virginia. Today about two-thirds of private land and four-fifths of natural wealth is owned by absentee resource corporations. In McDowell County, absentee landowners own 85% of the land and natural resources.[18]

In a wonderfully detailed and researched book by Ronald L. Lewis, *Transforming the Appalachian Countryside,* he notes that a tax commission report in 1884 stated that a state prospers when "those who permanently reside within her limits are increasing in wealth—if all the profits belong to persons who reside abroad—the state is going backwards."[19] Those pulling the money out will continue to be well fed. Those in state will go hungry. How long does it take to grasp this wisdom?

As Lewis writes, "In present West Virginia, little land was available for ordinary people after 1790." The goal of the speculators, the railroads, timber and coal industries was always the same: profit at the expense of the environment and people. Doing what is right and making a dollar have rarely been compatible in West Virginia. The coal companies use mountaintop removal to mine the coal as cheaply as possible with no regard for the future, just as timber companies of yesterday did in resorting to clear cutting as a way to reduce their costs. And today, because of tax breaks, the timber industry does not begin to pay a full share of the severance tax. They can afford to pay their way.[20]

Some respond—when offered the suggestion that there is a better way to mine the coal—that worker's compensation costs have made it necessary to mine the coal as cheaply as possible and to hell with the rest. "You just don't like coal," I was once told. One could sense the way to ruin friendships was to talk politics and religion, but if you really want to ruffle feathers nothing does it faster than questioning what coal has or has not done for the state. Coal is the sacred cow, and if you question it in some corners, you are "overreacting" and your nose "is in the air," you're a "know it all elitist," or a bureaucratic-pipe-smoking-tree sitter or a "frothy" soul who wants to chain himself to some piece of equipment in order to save our hills and dales. "Who needs another outsider telling us how to save ourselves? Only 'real' West Virginians who appreciate a good job understand why we need to continue blasting away the mountains."

The apologists for coal are not very interested in a moral argument, have no use for a sense of place unless it's a practical use—a make-money sense of place. Don't criticize unless you have solutions. This is fair. Solutions are not easy. But solutions first demand pulling heads out of the sand, taking the problems seriously and demanding what is only fair for the people. What can be done?

Supporting alternative energy research doesn't mean we have to stop mining coal. It doesn't mean convincing anyone to quit their job and go on the dole so that they can enjoy mountain beauty while contemplating their navel. It would be nice to see the people of the state benefit from what is left of coal. And is it unreasonable to mine coal in a responsible manner that emphasizes more than short-term gains?

We all have to deal with the hard facts of life. We all have our own moment of truth. West Virginia is facing such a moment. Congressman Nick Rahall is to be congratulated for finding money to help with the infrastructure of the southern mountains, but will those "magnificent" mountains and valleys be there for people to witness? Right now 41% of the streams are unfit, as are half the lakes. It seems as though the southern mountains have been given up as a lost cause, and fighting for them has been an exercise in frustration. The hard truth of reality will come in the last silent claim of freedom from the last standing fiercely independent and hungry mountaineer, and then what? We've all seen the hungry, the uneducated, the homeless, the ravaged land, and we have read the unending statistics. I think of the words, "Life, liberty, and justice for all" and "Mountaineers are always free." How did it happen? Why? Capitalism has let the people of West Virginia down.

Modernized mining hit its stride in the 1950s and 60s when the coal companies didn't want to pay high wages to so many miners. That left ghost towns. Between 1950 and 1970, West Virginia lost nearly 14% of its population. Twenty-seven of fifty-five counties lost population between 1990 and 2000. 2003 saw more jobs lost. My mother's birthplace in Brady, West Virginia, has long since been reclaimed by a scruffy wilderness. Her parents moved up the road to another coal community, Everttsville. But like many communities throughout West Virginia during the "boom era," it too has long been abandoned and is now extinct. The tiny houses were torn down and the land converted to a post-nuclear holocaust swamp created by the Army Corp of Engineers.

It is said that the coal boom period was one of prosperity. There's a coal boom right now in 2005. West Virginia in the first six months of 2004 was the 2nd highest coal-producing state. Is there prosperity? In 1917 there were something like 118 companies digging for bituminous coal in Raleigh County, West Virginia. I can't imagine there was ever prosperity in Brady, Maidsville, Cassville, Scott's Run, or Everttsville—though I know that Monongalia County was one of the richest areas for coal. It still produces a good amount, though in the county next-door, Marion, there is only one mine operating today.

Fatalism is what King Coal has always counted on, a kind of fatalism that says this is the way things are, the way things have been; there is nothing to be done and you should feel blessed for being born over a coal seam. The premises that Harry Caudill enumerates in his book regrettably hold true for West Virginia some forty years later. Welfare and state government are the largest supports of subsistence. Knowledge about today's job market is wanting. The schools are behind despite a coal company's annual teacher recognition award. Coal is still the tail wagging the dog.

The people don't like to rock the boat for fear of losing their livelihood. Though coal people will throw out numbers to back their case, the fact is that less than 3% of the state's job force is employed by mining.[21] However, the coal industry has affected every life in the state. Coal provides just enough money in tax revenues for the people and the state to hang themselves. For the state of West Virginia, coal is a sure route to suicide if the party structure remains against the people. Coal companies have fought unions from the beginning. Now the coal union has relatively few members. The disparity in wealth from coal owners to others is wider than ever.

Advanced mining technology means blowing up mountains ensuring that the patient—the mountains—will go quickly. Wallace Stegner writes of the west:

> *For mining I cannot say much good except that its operations are generally short lived. The extractable wealth is taken and the shafts, the tailings, and the ruins left, and in a dry country such as the American West the wounds men make in the earth do not quickly heal. Still, they are only wounds; they aren't absolutely mortal.* [22]

It is true that in parts of the world where the terrain is wild and far from populated areas, things can occur without witnesses and eventually nature heals as though nothing had happened. But in West Virginia's case, the wounds are mortal. The mountains will never recover.

Coal has been harshly criticized practically from the time the first coal seam was discovered. Coal has been a prime energy source and it powered us through World War II. My grandfather McIntyre, like thousands of others, was proud to be a miner, as were my uncles, and their reward was having their lives destroyed. Helen Pancake, mother of the West Virginia writer Breece D'J Pancake, told me, "When I saw coal-dust covered men coming home from work after being underground all day—I wanted to cry, they were extra special, super giants whose lives were so different from my rural farming communities of Frazier's Bottom, Hurricane and Milton; I didn't wonder at their wild spending and drinking."[23] Coal and West Virginia go hand in hand. But when widespread poverty and unemployment were brought about because of mechanization in the coal industry, I agreed with Jim Comstock, who wanted West Virginia to get up and get to work instead of "sitting around waiting for the second coming of John L. Lewis."

The resulting sorrow of seeing the wilderness leveled is an old story. The question is, will we hear the lessons that history has taught us? Why are we not hearing more about deforestation, soil erosion, and water management? What about our roads, schools, water supplies, hazardous waste clean up? There is some long overdue research being done with water in closed underground mines and the resulting effect on the surrounding environment.

Where does the Mining Engineering Department of West Virginia University stand? The Department's resources have been valuable for the coal industry. Do the engineers' and scientists' voices need to be louder in decrying what is happening in West Virginia? Is no one listening to them? Is everything hush-hush because the state would be bankrupt without the $300-400 million coal tax base? Are some researchers quiet because they are taking coal money for research? Are people tired of beating a dead horse because it is an old story with a predictable end? Why is funding for education in such dire straits? Why are state institutions being asked to take yet another funding cut? Has any coal company paid for an academic building at West Virginia University? There would seem to be a renaming opportunity for the right price with the Mineral Industries Building where Coal's Hall of Fame resides.

Part of my guilt lies in the fact that I am not there fighting on the front lines for what some consider expendable and others of us consider vital to our existence. There lies the rub. Again I defer to Stegner: "We simply need that wild country available to us, even if we never do more than drive to its edge and look in. For it can be a means of reassuring ourselves of our sanity as creatures, a part of the geography of hope."[24] Clean air laws passed in England in the 14th century made it a capital offense to burn coal in London. There is hope for the eastern half of the country to breathe easier in the years to come as the Clean Air Interstate Rule was issued from the EPA. But the political battle for clean air and water continues and will continue.

An acquaintance of mine is a proponent of Proposition 13 in California, which states that taxes can barely be raised on property owners who have owned their houses before, I think, 1976. All others must pay far higher taxes. Warren Buffet dared suggest that property taxes are too low in California and that proposition 13 should be readdressed. My acquaintance states, "We were here first, and I don't see why we should have to pay."

That's the mind-set that the mountains are up against—get yours while you can and to hell with everybody and everything else. You keep making the water filthy until it dies. You keep ignoring the fact that thousands of lives could be saved every year by not burning coal. You can still read the histories of Paint Creek or Cabin Creek. You can witness the devastation in Mingo and Logan Counties. My mother, who had nothing to apologize for, apologized for everything. Coal companies have everything to apologize for but apologize for nothing. We must teach our children that the kind of person a man is matters more than what he accumulates. Ironically this should be easy in a state where accumulation for the average working class West Virginian is very little.

The early isolation of people as a result of the mountains and the difficult travel helped to establish strong family bonds. That is also why families have been taken advantage of. Cut off from law and order and public scrutiny, exploiters have historically thought that no one will know or care.

In our fifth grade West Virginia history class, we learned to sing "The West Virginia Hills." For the southern counties and their people, it is now a bitter irony of a song. We need to start thinking about the land as home and care for it as such. We need to find a common ground beyond the quick judgment of right and wrong, beyond cause and effect, where we acknowledge that we are all one. Lincoln would be shocked to find the deplorable conditions that exist in parts of West Virginia. Jack Kennedy commented that he found it hard to believe the conditions that people were living under in West Virginia. Few people today in this country know what devastation is going on in the mountains of West Virginia.

For several years after leaving West Virginia, I mostly thought of it more as a concept than as an actuality. I mean as a place it was always rather idyllic, a gathering place for all those nostalgic souls who relished the familiarity and the smell of every nook and hollow. I also know that coal companies have won awards for reclamation and wildlife projects and that some coal people care as much as anyone about the environment. West Virginians have never worn rose-colored glasses. Their eyes have always seen with a hard realism. The coal industry says that hard realism requires mountaintop removal mining. They say the market doesn't support the old way of mining.

The abandoned coal communities around the state show the ghostly sting of how temporary life is. Lincoln's words "they shall not have died in vain" seem appropriate. This is the quandary that West Virginia finds itself in. With such ties to the past, how do we protect what the natives say they cherish, what they value most—the beauty and serenity of the place? How do we protect the earth while being pressured because of economics and a host of other unfathomable things, to change, to move ahead, to improve where the hand of man knows no restraints? Obliterating the mountains is not a good thing, and all the grass, shrubs and "viable" trees left behind will not convince me otherwise. We need to preserve what nature we can as a reminder of the past and a glimmer of what might have been, what still could be.

In our lifetimes we will go through 12,000 paper grocery bags, throw away 110,250 pounds of trash, and consume enough electricity to burn 16,610 pounds of coal. Many of those pounds of coal will come from West Virginia. Some pro-coal people ventured that these mountains weren't good for anything, people couldn't live on them, and they weren't even fit for goats. That's one way to look at it. The mountains were not necessarily meant for human habitation, but to be appreciated and protected with respect and awe.

Coal executives say that the flattened mountains in southern West Virginia make nice shopping malls, golf courses, and parks. If they could bring back Frederick Olmsted, the landscape architect who designed Central Park in New York City, I might be persuaded. Who is going to visit these fanciful parks? Who is going to pay for the infrastructure? It is true and hardly news that West Virginia does not have an abundance of flat land to develop. Certainly one of West Virginia's problems in economic development terms has been its terrain.

But the big problem—as noted by Barbara Rasmussen—is that in many counties absentee and federal ownership of a vast portion of the land occurs. So not only do the residents not control the wealth, they can't tax it. The idea that the coal industry is doing the state a favor by creating "beautiful, rounder" plateaus of flat land for development taxes common sense—especially when as of this writing in the last thirty years only 2% of the leveled land has been used for any development. I guess a high population large city could magically appear on some of that flat land created by mountaintop mining removal, along with an international airport. Are golf courses and shopping malls what we need or want instead of land that was meant for the ages?

Mountains are a pleasure—ask any West Virginian, ask most anyone from anywhere. Most people see a place differently, but I dare say that most West Virginians see their mountains through the same eyes. Some people, like my father, after reaching adulthood and having no time to spare, may have had no desire or time to hike the mountain peaks. That may even mean they have no interest in great vistas. They may never even contemplate the mountains, but, like Dad, some folks just like to know the mountains are there, that they are not going to be raped and left behind like roadkill.

In a state that has been indoctrinated toward coal, it is noteworthy that a recent poll of state residents, taken by the Appalachian Center for the Economy and the Environment, showed that 56% oppose mountaintop mining, with 26% in favor.

DAVID SELBY

Mountain top removal in Wyoming County, WV. Courtesy Robert F. Gates/Omni Productions

You can simply look at a mountain and feel refreshed. Nature soothes the soul.

It is hard to pull the politicians of West Virginia together to stop the coal companies. A century old habit of being weak and submissive is hard to break. Scott Russell, in *Writing From The Center*, says:

> *The framers of the Constitution may have assumed that we did not need a Bill of Responsibilities because religion and reason and the benign impulses of our nature would lead us to care for one another and for our home. At the end of a bloody century, on the eve of a new millennium that threatens to be still bloodier, few of us now feel much confidence in those redeeming influences.* [25]

How ironic and sad that there should be such a disregard for people in a place where patriotism flows in service to our country, where veterans and enlistments are among the nation's highest.

My father doesn't know too much about the "mountaintop removal" story. But he trusts me when I tell him about it, and though he wonders whether this is just more left wing propaganda, he is won over when I show him pictures. He shakes his head. He looks at the pictures again. "Disgusting," he says. "Life there will never be the same. We should be ashamed." Yes we should, Dad. We have sold the mountain's dignity, broken our vow to protect, and in turn it may all come back to haunt us. There is a long silence. Finally Dad says, "Hard to believe; there's got to be another way."

8

THOSE DAMN FACTS AND FIGURES

If there is a mountain that needs to be toppled, it is the seemingly never-ending mountain of depressing facts and figures about West Virginia. The picture is a fairly miserable one and one that has been fairly consistent over the years. As Lincoln said, "The time will never come when the people won't know exactly what sugar-coated means."

The United States—the wealthy superpower that we are—is not in the top ten countries (in fact is far from it) for most of the important categories like health, childhood poverty, literacy, mathematical literacy, and infant mortality, so West Virginia's dismal showing must be seen in that context.

West Virginia is fairly racially homogenous, about 94% white. Not surprisingly, it ranks last in percentage of foreign language speakers—98% speak English only. Most minorities live in a four-county area. African Americans played a large role in the history of West Virginia coalfields, and their ancestors deserve attention. As an ethnic group in West Virginia, African Americans rank lower than others in every meaningful ranking. No wonder the black population is decreasing. West Virginia black infant mortality is 21.6% compared to a white rate of 6.7%. For every 100 black students enrolled in college in West Virginia, 11 receive a degree.

It is noteworthy that 70% of black students graduate high school in West Virginia. That's better than in New York. According to the *New York Post*, West Virginia holds black students to a higher standard, and the students respond. Why then are so many not completing their college degrees? It is not necessarily racial prejudice that is the problem; it is to some extent perhaps a problem of black culture—influence of peers; fewer college-educated role models. The problem is also pure economics. The state has the 2nd highest poverty rate—the state needs more money for low-income children to go to school. Twenty-eight percent of all children in West Virginia live in poverty—the fourth highest figure in the nation. The situation is thankfully improving, as West Virginia is investing more today in its children because it knows first hand that childhood poverty leads to a road of failure.

We all want our lives to count for something. West Virginia's needs give a real meaning to improving the state's quality of life. One of the most practical things that West Virginians can do for their state and country is vote. More than a third of the nation's voters didn't show up to vote in the presidential election of 2004. West Virginia is ranked 46th nationwide in voter turnout for women. It ranks 46th in the number of women holding any kind of elected office. West Virginia women are strong, but they have let the men have their way at the voting booth. When women have voted, they have not supported women for public office. Women's income and employment ranks 51st—which includes Washington, DC. One reason is that the jobs available in West Virginia do not employ women.[1]

My mother's mother loaded coal on a locomotive, but this was a rare thing for women. They were mostly confined to service jobs like my father's mother, who was a domestic. The possibility that mountaineer women will reach parity with men in pay and employment is not probable in the foreseeable future (though the gap is narrowing). Unpaid labor, such as gardening, baking and making clothes, was and is the women's tradition.

West Virginia is consistently among the top three states in the nation for obesity. There is a health crisis in the state, which the state has acknowledged by calling in the federal disease investigators. West Virginia ranks 49th in social and economic autonomy and health and well-being for women. Women in West Virginia are the most likely in the country to die of heart disease. They rank 50th in smoking, 49th and 50th for lung cancer and diabetes, and 50th for obesity and dental visits. They have one of the lowest rates of abortion in the nation, but only 16% live in counties with abortion providers. Teenage pregnancy is above the national average, where one-third of all U.S. children are born out of wedlock.

West Virginia women have the lowest level of education in the country. The status of women in a state made up of strong women is abysmal. In some counties, yardsticks such as early marriage, poor diet, and domestic violence, to name a few, are comparable to the Third World. A recent grant to West Virginia University will hopefully raise the standard of women's health in the state. But it will take a concerted effort on many fronts to help West Virginia women realize their dreams. It requires people willing to lend a hand, perhaps to sacrifice a bit for the good of all, perhaps plowing a larger portion of coal, timber, and other industry money back into the state.

West Virginia ranks near the bottom for high school graduation. Bachelor degree numbers are very low, and though more high school seniors are going to college—56.5% in 2004—West Virginia ranks near the bottom for high school graduation. The percentage of young adults aged 18-34 who enroll in college level education has dropped significantly.[2] On the plus side, student test scores are on the rise. There are more very good and qualified teachers, but their pay is among the nation's lowest, and the student-teacher ratio is getting worse. Parents are not involved nearly enough with their children's schools. The state schools, in worse shape than half a century ago, need $1.3 billion for modernization. West Virginia spends more on busing kids around than any other state—with 36% of the roads in poor condition. The West Virginia traffic fatality rate is 50% higher than the national average.

West Virginia leads the nation in percentage of persons 16 to 19 who are idle, meaning not in school and not working. Poverty and a lack of education are roadblocks to a person's self-respect and confidence. How do we develop programs that will offer opportunities for these young people to feel useful? Even if such programs are volunteer ones, they could serve as a road to a feeling of self-worth. The obvious alternate road is one of pleasure through drugs. West Virginia ranks 47th in the country for state prison incarcerations; 56.2 % of federal sentences are drug related. Hundreds of millions of dollars have been spent on drug abuse programs.

West Virginia ranks lowest in foreign investment, technology in schools and job creation. By 1998, service jobs—like in the food and beverage sector with low pay and no benefits—overtook coal-mining jobs. Some feel that growth will come from a knowledge-based economy; but in the high-tech spectrum, West Virginia ranks 50th in the nation. It suffers failing grades in business vitality and development capacity. The ten fastest growing jobs pay an average of $26,009. Those fresh out of college with a bachelor's degree make an average of $25,000 if they stay in West Virginia. West Virginia loses 20% of its young, single, well-educated adults—the fourth highest number in the nation. It has been put forth by some that as an economic boost we can import everybody's garbage and nuclear waste—we can bury them under the lopped off mountain waste from mountaintop mining. There is currently an out-of-state company that wants to dump huge amounts of garbage into McDowell County.

West Virginia is last in housing construction, even though Dad says that "houses are springing up everywhere like weeds—'bout as attractive too." Housing value in West Virginia is last in the country. Many housing units are substandard with no running water, no indoor plumbing, unsafe wiring and no insulation. West Virginia is ranked 47th in sewage treatment needs. It is in the bottom ten for toxic releases and greenhouse gas emissions. Medicare for the disabled is the highest in the nation. West Virginia has the lowest rank for prevention and duration of carpal tunnel cases. It leads the country in obesity, more strokes, more lung disease, heart disease, unintentional injuries, and suicides. People in West Virginia smoke more, and sit around more. The latter is ironic considering its great outdoors makes it the 2nd most rural state in the nation.

Smokeless tobacco use is the highest in the nation. In West Virginia, male teenagers are twice as likely to use smokeless tobacco than any other male teens in the country. Every West Virginian pays $359.00 each year for health care costs due to smoking.[3] A higher tobacco tax was imposed that should help with the budget. If it weans some people off tobacco, it might save the state health care dollars. Annual health care costs caused by smoking are $636 million. Forty percent of the people can't afford health care or because of a lack of transportation can't get to a health care provider. Still, emergency room visits are the highest in the nation—37% higher than the national average.

West Virginians take 40% more prescription drugs than the national average. There is a lack of social services in rural areas and a shortage of mental health services. Health care for children is appalling. And of course the population is older than in most states—15% are 65 and older, which means a lot of social security recipients. There are only two workers for every retiree, and there are more deaths than births.[4] The older population brings its own problems, such as the highest rate of diabetes in the country. Diabetes isn't helped, of course, by having about the worst diet in the country.

West Virginia is the third most forested state in the nation. In 1994 the timber cut was more than double the 1987 amounts. Only 3% of the forest are protected. So today West Virginia is in danger of repeating its history as it struggles again with deforestation, soil erosion, and an increasing arid landscape from mismanagement and disregard from state leaders. The state has about the coldest economy in the nation despite recent big profits for coal and timber. It ranks 48th in the nation in total state and local taxes and fees on a per capita basis. Its tax capacity is the 5th lowest in the nation, and poor families are hit harder in West Virginia by an income tax than those in most other states.[5] The food tax should be eliminated. God bless gas taxes and the lottery, but there are obvious risks in depending on gambling revenues. Not surprisingly West Virginia is near the bottom in charitable contributions. West Virginia has the lowest rural income per capita. Income is far below the national average—in the 2000 census West Virginia ranked 50th per capita income. Overall, 19.3% of people live in poverty—second highest in the country. In McDowell County, 37.7 % live in poverty, despite mining more coal than any other county in the state. McDowell County also has the highest adult illiteracy in the state. But then the United States is 49th in the world in literacy.

In the Eastern Panhandle, Jefferson County, with a median income of $44,374, is middle class in a poor state. Berkeley and Jefferson counties of West Virginia have the best employment, and along with Morgan and Hampshire are the fastest growing places in the state—though Berkeley and Jefferson also have one of the highest high school dropout rates in the state. Some want to put a stop to all the uncontrolled "growth" in what have become bedroom communities for people who work in Washington, DC and other cities in Virginia and Maryland, where the cost of housing goes up every month. The Eastern Panhandle of West Virginia is a nice place to live, and it's comparatively cheap.

Despite the current governor's statements that "our workers are the best in the world...a work force that is as skilled as it is dedicated" and "our quality of life is unsurpassed," such basement-ranking statistics of basically every positive indicator don't lie. The state's poverty, poor education, and feelings of neglect breed suspicion and anger. West Virginia has consistently ranked near the bottom in all areas that have to do with the welfare of its people. What do the faces behind the numbers look like? They are just as anxious and willing and eager to please as the Latino men on the curb in L.A. In the end, although life has certainly been a struggle for many mountaineers, most would not want to live anywhere else. In fact, relatively more people—like my mother and father—proportionally spend their entire lives in West Virginia than in any other state.

West Virginia officials are aware of the many problems and are seeking answers. Present Governor Manchin and the legislature are to be congratulated for increasing the severance tax to help meet the state's obligations. It is a start for a debt long overdue. Money is an issue. It behooves the state to use its natural resources wisely and to get every penny the people deserve from the selling of those resources—especially if southern West Virginia is going to be sacrificed in the process.

9

HOMETOWN

If you take Interstate 79 south out of Pittsburgh, Pennsylvania, an hour and a half of soft rolling hills later you will be in northern West Virginia. A few miles later, you will see the exit sign for Morgantown, WV. If you turn left you come to the once booming coal camp of Osage. To the right is Morgantown, otherwise known as "Touchdown City," positive thinking on behalf of the fans of West Virginia University's football team. I find it all serendipitous because the very first football team in 1891 was partly financed with proceeds from a student production of Shakespeare's *Richard III*.

Morgantown was and is a nice—if one overlooks the state of student housing which seems to me to be in dire need of an undercover investigation—functional working class college town on the banks of the Monongahela River, named by native Americans for its muddy banks. Monongalia County was formed in 1776 by an act of the Virginia General Assembly. At one time it was about as large as a third of the present state of West Virginia, but was greatly reduced with the creation of other counties and the extension of the Mason Dixon line, which left three counties in Pennsylvania.

Morgantown was established in 1785 by the General Assembly of the State of Virginia, having been surveyed back in 1774 by one Zackquill Morgan. His namesake had been an educational center long before the Civil War. A local academy established in 1814 had 176 students from 14 states in 1854. Then the Agricultural College of West Virginia was established. The name was changed in 1868 to West Virginia University. Even then we were concerned with image. Some probably thought that the name change would help the perception that the school was not as prestigious as others.

The university was a beacon of light for me. But this would

not have been true if my parents had not been willing to work to improve their lives. They truly were in Lincoln's words "prudent, penniless beginner(s)."[1] My mother left her coal camp community of Brady and my father left the farm. There have been hints that Dad felt somewhat isolated on the farm where he grew up. He recalled walking to school ten miles each way. It was dark when he left for school and dark when he returned. And the fact that he left the farm and never returned to live, except for the period while he was building our house in town, was not all my mother's idea. Dad wished to get away from farm responsibilities, such as tending a garden. He wanted to set out on his own, away—but not too far away—from the family circle. Once he got away, he never planted a garden or hunted or did any of the things that were required of a farm boy.

The move to Morgantown must have felt to my parents like I felt when leaving West Virginia. Mom always said that one generation works to provide a better life for the next. Again Lincoln wrote: "While we reverence their memory, let us not forget how vastly greater is our opportunity."[2] My opportunities were vastly greater because my parents decided to live in Morgantown, even though, excepting for the university, it was somewhat geographically and culturally isolated. Mom and Dad knew it would be a good hometown, a good place to grow up, and a good place for daydreaming. I left my hometown at a time in the mid-sixties when many young people were leaving the state. Though I no longer get butterflies when returning to my hometown, I still have a feeling of ease, warmth, and "rootedness." Dad recently said to me: "You do like it here." Yes, Dad, I do. I like having a hometown, roots, and knowing that there was something decent and good about it. Good things rubbed off and helped make me, I trust, a better person because Morgantown provided me with a solid foundation. Long ago, this place got me moving; it gave me sustenance for the road, and for that I am eternally grateful.

In their way, all small towns, no matter how idyllic, are probably just as provincial and common as my hometown or most hometowns, urban or not. The things that bind us to them can be elusive but necessary. I knew every apple and cherry tree in my neighborhood. Long ago, I went looking for them, and of course they were all gone. In a way, it doesn't matter that they are gone, for they are in my memory, and that seems to be an ever-growing part of my world. Some of us can't wait to leave the hometown, and some of us never want to leave, and I suppose some want to leave but for whatever reasons can't, or some simply never get around to leaving. Of those who leave, some never go back, and some make annual pilgrimages back. Some of us try to return though we may know better, and some of us are glad we did even if the magic has long gone—though the past is quite alive.

No matter if you stay or leave your hometown, I agree with Stegner that there is a time for a child when he or she is branded for life and try if you want, you can never shed that early environment. It is with me in the way I talk and walk, in how the seasons of the year affect me, in the things I value, in my sense of right and wrong, my independence, my insecurities, weaknesses, affectations, prejudices, innocence, fears, my love of nature, gardens, my appreciation for the good things of life—a fire, a rocker, a good apple, a good story, good friends, the joy of hard work; all these helped form the essence of who I am. Most of all, I owe whatever character I have to my mother and father and my hometown, but especially to my West Virginia wife, the person I have shared most of my life with, the one who has been with me all the way, the one who knows.

When Mom and Dad decided in the late 1930s to make their lives "in town," Morgantown was booming. They must have been excited for the future, not realizing their lives were to change in 1941. Dad's security guard job at DuPont was draft-exempt; but he—as most others did—enlisted in World War II. Coal companies and DuPont—which after World War II became Olin-Matheson—were, along with the University, the big employers. DuPont had rushed its Morgantown plant into production because of the war. It manufactured ammonia needed for explosives. While Dad was in the Navy, Mom and I lived in a small apartment at the top of South Park Hill, which I later would associate as the wealthier part of town, or at least where a lot of the doctors, lawyers, and professors lived.

Our landlord was Bill Malcolm. Bill was a barber who gave me most every haircut till I left Morgantown. At the conclusion of every haircut, Bill would give me a head rub; then he would take my ears, give them a couple of tugs and let his thumbs go around my ears and down behind them to my shoulders. It gave me a tingle every time. Bill was a smoker—a couple of clips, couple of puffs, couple of coughs, and a couple of laughs. He even taught his dog to smoke. He trained the dog to water ski, too. Bill was a wonder on water skis, but the best was to see his dog sitting up on a ski, flying through the water at Cheat Lake. But the funniest trick in those days was to watch that dog puff away on a cigarette. Bill died of lung cancer. I don't know about the dog; he may have drowned. It is the people you love, people like Bill, a West Virginian through and through, who want nothing more than to not just be written about, made assumptions about, but to be seen anew—seen as most West Virginians see, with the heart.

Mom and I were constant companions during the years Dad was in the war. She didn't have a car and couldn't drive anyway, so we walked everywhere. Morgantown was a place where you could do without a car. South Park Hill was a hill I came to dread. Funny how I only thought of hills as something I would have to climb. It was a fun walk down, a long walk back up. A short time before her death Mom talked briefly about a trip we took to New York to see Dad. He was based at the Brooklyn Naval Yard. She recalled the place we stayed and the mice that ruled the nights—she was afraid to sleep.

Upon returning from the Navy and World War II, Dad had, unlike some other returning vets, no desire to ever leave West Virginia again. He had no desire for another life. It was a good time to be home in West Virginia. Although the atomic bomb was the new invention and people worried that there was now the means to destroy the globe, this couldn't diffuse the country's optimism and neither could McCarthy and Russia, although both got under the skin of America. A couple of years after the war, I had a baby brother, Craig, and we had a brand new house. In 1949 there was a new car, a wine-red Plymouth that all the neighbors came to see. Life was good. Man came out of the dark of World War II with a renewed hope, holding on to the sense that goodness had not perished. Out of this new environment, my father and grandfather built our house.

Dad was electrician, plumber, and carpenter. He dug the foundation, laid the block, cut every board and hammered every nail in the house that he still owns today. Mom was ever present, holding a board with the aid of the sawhorses and constantly sweeping up clouds of sawdust. Together they molded a place with their hearts and labor that at one time seemed as permanent as their marriage. Dad and Grandpap framed the house with two-by-fours, real two-by-fours that had been cut from trees that in turn had been cut off Grandpap's farm, felled by hand with a crosscut saw. Horses were used to skid the logs out of the woods. Then they were loaded onto an old truck and hauled to the sawmill that Grandpap and Dad built at the farm powered by a Studebaker engine that Dad and Grandpap got from a junkyard. The trees were laid and locked on a wide belt that carried them into a saw blade three to four feet in diameter. The sawmill's most distinctive feature was a huge slab pile that eventually amassed below the mill, finally reaching thirty feet or so in the air. I loved to walk around on it until it was discovered that it was a haven for copperheads and rattlesnakes.

The new house cost $5,000 to build. How did Dad know how to build a house? He had never built one before. If you can build a house, you can build a life. Not many of us get to build a house or perhaps even want to. But in one way or another we are, if we are fortunate, involved with making a home. Habitat for Humanity, the organization that organizes volunteers to build houses, is aptly titled. Houses are places where people live and grow, and ideally they provide a haven from the elements. There is warmth from a furnace—fireplaces today are mostly atmospheric—and a bed to lie in. I remember the amount of time Mom and Dad took to pick out the front door; and finally when it was put in place, where it still resides today, the home seemed complete.

In a childhood scrapbook of Dad's that he gave me, there is the cutout picture of a fairly large brick house. Dad's childhood dream house was larger than his future small modest one with wood siding painted white. Before Mom and Dad got too old to paint it, they covered it with aluminum. There were originally two bedrooms, a living room, a nice kitchen with cheery wood cabinets, and an indoor bathroom. Later the attic and basement

The author with his brother, Craig.

were finished, adding two bedrooms and a small family room with one of the original bedrooms being turned into a dining area. Mom and Dad did all the remodeling while I was a sophomore in college living at home. I was a "sometime" helper. The house wasn't greedy in its use of space. The neighbors' houses were only five feet or so away on each side. Our house was maybe five miles from the farm where Dad grew up and a world away from the coal camp of Mom's youth. It provided the basics of a nice place to eat and sleep, to put your feet up—as long as your shoes were off— and take refuge from burdens.

There is no way to describe what my father's house means to him. Only he knows what the house says to him. Only he can truly see the oak and cherry stains that he and Mom hand-rubbed into each hand-cut oak doorframe, each piece of flooring, each kitchen cabinet. C. G. Jung said about the stone tower retreat that he built where he felt he was most deeply himself:

> *There is nothing in the Tower that has not grown into its own form over the decades, nothing with which I am not linked. Here everything has its history, and mine; here is space for the spaceless kingdom of the world's and the psyche's hinterland...*[3]

This is how many West Virginians feel about the place where they live. It is more than on-call transportation, air conditioning, fm radio, and satellites. It is more than Nike shoes and CD's, more than TiVo and DVD's. It is the continuum of life.

The neighborhood where our house was located was called Woodburn, a middle class section of Morgantown. It had everything you needed, including Friends' Grocery Store where our family had the important and needed credit account. Flo Sanders, the pretty checker—whose family owned Sanders Dairy from where bottled milk was delivered to our door twice a week and during the cold winters the cream would rise lifting the cap right off the bottle—let me charge dimes to my parents' account so that I could buy a soda across the street at the beer-on-tap confectionary. The confectionary was where all the neighborhood children drank soda, read comic books, and eventually graduated to beer and racy magazines like *Gold Nugget* and *Sexology*. Tom and Ann Torch, the owners, watched us start grade school and saw most of us finish college. It was there you got to watch Dewey Gall drink egg in his beer. Except for Dewey and a few others, most serious beer drinkers were across the road at another smaller bar that didn't have comic books and milk shakes and so had no children. Connors Cleaners was where I took old wire hangers for redemption, two for a penny.

The Ashland Oil gas station, which Dad leased for a couple of years and lost his shirt because he gave credit to everybody and hired a worker who put more money in his pocket than in the cash drawer, was where we got our gas. I learned to grease and change oil in a car there. There was Henderson's car shop for serious repairs. There was a bakery where I worked infrequently making doughnuts before the sun rose and a barbershop where butcher Dan the barber man plied his trade and cut my hair—once.

Running down the hill from the red-bricked Woodburn grade school at three in the afternoon left the rest of the day for "hide and seek," "kick the can," or "thirty scatter." Only Mother's call to dinner could end my day in the street.

We played touch football or basketball in the street with a straw basket nailed to the telephone pole where hardly a game was interrupted by a car. Old Mr. Phillips drove so slowly we would call time out for a drink. He was the kind man who drove me to the hospital after a bike wreck. The joke was it was a wonder I didn't bleed to death before we got there.

Cheat Lake, where the Cheat River empties, sits peacefully at the bottom of Coopers Rock, which sits atop Cheat Mountain. At some point in time, the bed at the base of Cooper's Rock was flooded, and Cheat Lake took life. It became the recreation spot for the town of Morgantown. There was swimming and boating in the summer and ice-skating in the winter. Cheat River got its name from "cheating" so many out of their lives. It almost got mine when a tall skinny redhead, Eddie Utzman, snuck up behind me and pushed me in. My secret of not knowing how to swim was out in short order. I was already going down for the third time, and my life up to that time truly passed through me. It took the strength of my three friends, Butch, Eddie, and Walt, who all years later were ushers in my wedding—to save me. They

Eddie, Walt, me and Butch.

nearly drowned while pulling me ashore. Later the boy who pushed me in seemed as frightened as I had been. "Jesus, Selby, I didn't know you couldn't swim." I still can't. I can't even float.

In winter there were snow and hills for sledding. There were plentiful seasonal berries and apples, plums, peaches, cherries, assorted nuts, all sorts of goodies for a hungry child to pick at will. You had to work to earn great vistas by hiking to the top of a mountain, but the reward was a wind-swept view to the next mountain that let me wonder about what was on the other side. As a young boy, there was nothing more exciting for me than packing a peanut butter sandwich and hiking to a green spot on a hill spotted from another hill. On arriving I thought I had to have been the first human to step foot on the place. I would lay prone high on a green patch where there was no time and the mind was as cloudless as the rich blue sky, and no peanut butter sandwich ever tasted so good, especially when washed down with cool spring water from an old army canteen that was hooked on my army belt.

Then with a west wind blowing me on and on toward the sunset, taking me far beyond my intended destination, I would suddenly grow anxious realizing that there was no way to get back home before dark. I would tell myself not to let my imagination run away with me. But when night fell and the woods turned dark, the trees took on ominous shapes and personalities. Forest sounds turned eerie as the woods seemed to get more mysterious and the trees talked and groaned and complained in whispers, and I would run to home as fast as I could.

At times I still run, trying to recapture those innocent days. There was no thought of being stereotyped or being denied anything. There was nothing Appalachian to overcome. I was hardly aware of people of "higher status." There was the Morgantown Country Club—long gone—replaced by other nearby clubs and resorts. Because of the university, Morgantown was and is an oasis in West Virginia. It is more prosperous than most other areas of the state and holds the potential to become West Virginia's leading city.

Most boys who grew up in West Virginia had at least an acquaintance with hunting and fishing, which some families depended on to supplement their meals. My family was ambivalent about hunting and fishing, partly because we were not dependent on game and fish for our meals. My father rarely hunted and never fished. He never showed me how to shoot or hunt. I felt a little inadequate at not being a hunter. I recall only once as a boy of eight or nine going out to the farm to hunt squirrels. I didn't carry a gun, and Dad didn't bag a single squirrel that day. He would not be concerned that I wouldn't bring any squirrel tails home to hang on the car antenna. Dad had a soft wool red plaid hunting outfit Mom got for him from Sears and Roebuck. I have the jacket to it today, and when I'm somewhere in the mountains where it's cold enough, I wear it—feeling somewhat like an actor in his costume, but at least briefly I look like a hunter.

Except for occasionally breaking a neighbor's window, I was a kid who couldn't get into trouble because there was no trouble to get into. Lots of unsettling things were percolating during these so-called innocent years, but the fears and troubles of my childhood for the most part were self-inflicted. Mostly it was cakewalks and May pole dances and fall festivals and cub scouts and baseball. Oh, I did manage to take a cookie from one of the cookie bins of Albright's store while Miss Albright was in the back slicing some lunchmeat. But no one knew except probably Miss Albright. The 1950s meant pink shirts with the collar rolled up and black pants. As a young boy, I wanted to be able to wear Levi's like some other boys. I wanted to peg the pants so that the dark blue stripe showed just so when the cuff was rolled up. I remember so clearly when I had saved six or seven dollars and went to buy my first pair of Levi's at the army-navy store on Pleasant Street in Morgantown. I lament that they no longer make a single pair of Levi's in this country.[4]

Baseball was the sport. It truly was the national pastime. Every little town had a baseball team. In northern West Virginia, the people rooted for the Pittsburgh Pirates; the southern part of the state lived and died with the Cincinnati Reds; the Eastern Panhandle held out for the old Washington Senators. Baseball was a working person's game, one that brought my family and others a great deal of enjoyment—including my mother-in-law, who listened to the Cincinnati Reds while she sewed. As a child, the Pirates were my team. Ralph Kiner was the home run hitter, and Roberto Clemente was the great hitter and right fielder, Bob Friend and Vernon Law the pitchers, and the great Elroy Face the reliever. I hardly missed hearing a game and actually got to go to old Forbes Field once to see them play. But the best was listening to Rosy Roswell, the Pirate's announcer. He would announce the games on a slight delay via ticker tape. Every time a Pirate hit a home run, Rosy would call out, "Open the window, Aunt Minny, here she comes."

My career as a baseball player crash-landed when I faced a hard-throwing pitcher, Jim Ponceroff, who later signed a minor league contract as I recall with the Phillies. I never came close to getting a hit off Jim because I was standing so far off home plate thinking of self-preservation. He and Tommy Shaffer, who had a mean curve ball and who signed with the Yankees, were the premier pitchers in our town back then. I did manage once to get a lucky single off the curve baller. My favorite team was the Yankees, not because they seemed to always win but because Gene Corum, a football coach at West Virginia University and friend of my parents, had gotten Casey Stengel's autograph signed to my brother and me. It is framed along with a few other Yankee items and adorns a wall in our home.

The year Casey signed his autograph for us was 1953; the year the Yankees won their fourth World Series in a row. It was a record the 2001 Yankees were trying to equal. They came up just short but more importantly they helped lift the spirits of millions whose lives had abruptly changed on September 11, 2001. Millions of people cheered, laughed, cried and were thankful as they watched the Yankees represent their city with everything they could give. The series between the Yankees and Diamondbacks may have been the best I have ever seen. It seemed both teams were determined to give every ounce of talent and energy and heart in playing those games, assuring that America's home was still vibrant and alive. I was grateful for that 2001World Series because it took me back to a time where the grass was green and the mind free of care. I hope that some of today's young were just as taken with it as I was.

One of the first things I remember seeing, I believe in 1952, on our first blond cabinet Dumont (I think it was so named) black and white television set was an H-bomb test. Television, except for *Howdy Doody* and westerns, was not a big thing in my early childhood. The early Saturday morning shoot 'em up Westerns were a must. Lash LaRue, Tex Ritter, Gene Autry, Roy Rogers and Gabby Hayes and the Lone Ranger were favorites. I had my picture taken with Smiley Burnette, who was always a sidekick to the hero. He appeared at the local Oaks Drive-in. The cowboys were my first heroes. I would slap the side of my leg and yell "gidda up" to my fantasy horse. I had a pair of silver six-shooters as a first grader. I would practice my draw and spinning the guns around my fingers and back into their black holsters. They were the only guns I have ever owned.

Dick Clark with his *American Bandstand* was a favorite when I was a teenager. *The Honeymooners, Lassie, Life With Riley, Father Knows Best*, and *Ozzie And Harriet*, all had their place in my growing up. *Sky King* was a big show. I sent away for his ring and wore it proudly. The shows had nothing to do with my world, though if we weren't like those folks on TV, perhaps we wanted to be. In time television would reshape how life was lived, even in West Virginia. During the fifties we were very good at keeping unpleasant things at bay. I loved *Robin Hood, Martin and Lewis* and *Shane*—though I cried at *Shane*. I loved *Gone With the Wind, High Noon*, and anything Jimmy Stewart was in. In truth I guess I loved all movies except the scary ones. I have yet to see *The Exorcist, The Shining* or even *Jaws*, and *Scream* is definitely out. Somehow those films are too real for me.

When my children were young, there was Mr. Rogers of public television fame, whom my wife and I enjoyed as much as our children did. His opening little song always gave me a warm feeling of assuredness as gentle as a soft rain. I felt cozy and safe with cookies and a glass of milk curled up on the couch with a light silent snow falling outside and my children wrapped in a blanket beside me. Perhaps it was Fred Rogers' voice, so easy, friendly, talking to just me. I don't know if repeats of Mr. Rogers' neighborhood were on in the days following September 11; I didn't think to see. I should have. I needed him. All children do. John Cleese's *Faulty Towers*—a far cry from Mr. Rogers—but also shown on PBS television, (I have the tapes) is as good a remedy for me today as any for bringing joy to darker times.

It was radio that played the important role in my younger years, consuming me from the time I would come in from play to long after I should have been asleep. My green Zenith radio's little lighted "Z" kept me company. It was radio that fired my imagination, allowing me to see whatever in my mind's eye: the sleek green car of the *The Green Hornet*, the trench-coated agents in *FBI, Peace and War*, or *The Shadow*, which tingled my spine. I could really see the *Shadow's* shadow and believed that "only the shadow knows." The creaky door of *Inner Sanctum* scared both Mom and me. It was over the top the way the radio announcer gave us "Bobbie Benson And The B-Bar B-eeeeee!" But you couldn't wait for it to start. And that was true for the vast snow-covered Yukon of Sergeant Preston and his dog, King. I loved the music of *Johnny Diamond, Private Detective*, and the phone ringing to announce *Dr. Christian's Office*. Then there was the unforgettable, wonderful laugh of *The Great Gildersleeve*. To this day, *The Jack Benny Show* and *Burns and Allen* bring inner warmth and a smile. *Amos and Andy, Fibber McGee and Molly* . . . so many wonderful shows combined to play a part in the formation of home.

Living in Morgantown in the fifties, life seemed nothing if not hopeful. No one talked about the Korean War. Although Dad's brother was serving in Korea, I never heard much mention of that conflict. In contrast, a few years later television allowed the Vietnam War and racial unrest to play nonstop in our living rooms. Children today know about terrorists. Though I was nervous about "the bomb" and communism, there were no real graphic images of war in our neighborhood. As a child, if it was dark and I was alone, what you couldn't see was far more frightening. I had never heard of murder, even the word. We never locked our door. It was the fifties! In my youth no one I ever knew had been kidnapped or sexually abused or robbed or shot. No one got lost. Parents did not get divorced. You married for life. All was seemingly right with the world.

Being ignorant about the hard realities of life for many people, it took awhile for me to realize that if you were African American, the jobs were limited to the coal mines, hauling trash, shining shoes, or being the doorman at the Hotel Morgan, the only hotel in town. There was Eddie Doon's hamburger place, with the best hamburger I've ever eaten. Mr. Doon was African American ("colored" back then). It was rumored he had a secret hamburger recipe. Nearing high school graduation a boy—who later played quarterback for Army—said of my friend Charles Blue, a "colored" boy who was all-state in four sports, but did not receive any scholarship offers, "High school's a short career." It was if you were colored, I would later learn. Chuck and I became friends in the eighth grade when segregation was ended in the schools, and we were put in the same homeroom where we won the class sporting championship—thanks to Chuck. Till then I had had no idea or understanding about where Chuck had previously gone to school. I started to sense that something was insidiously wrong when I would hide and watch a black classmate, Bill White, pick up my family's garbage. As a youngster in Morgantown, I was not yet aware of discrimination.

There was zero tolerance of anything that smacked of being

abnormal. That was the ugly part of the fifties and, I guess, of youthful worlds in general. There was the occasional taunting and harassment and young macho attitude front you had to put up as a result. My uneasiness paled when I thought about the indignities that "homos" and "retards" and the "coloreds" had to put up with. A teacher's slightest careless remark can be remembered a lifetime later. That I was not allowed to escort the May Queen in junior high I suppose did me no great harm; but I remember the slight and the embarrassment when told, "You would fall down." The remark was typical of that teacher, who used words as verbal terrorism.

Then there was the vice-principal, who patrolled the halls like Richard III. The junior high gym teacher one day hollered at me when I tripped running down the basketball court, "Get up, slewfoot." I was admittedly not the most graceful of players and was noted for tripping over my feet, but he never thereafter called me anything but "slew-foot." Maybe the teacher was right in not allowing me to be an escort; I very well might have fallen down, but I would have gotten back up, and who knows, with a little encouragement, I might have danced. Young West Virginians need to be encouraged to dance.

My first twelve years of schooling were generally misspent. There was no one to blame but myself. My teachers were, on the whole, warm and wonderful. My best year was in the third grade. It was because of our teacher, Mrs. Cordray, a bird-like, tall woman who once called Jack Dorenze and me (Jack was later killed in a coal mine) into the coatroom for a paddling. She proceeded to paddle a stack of books and told us to act like our "hineys" hurt and sent us back into the classroom instructing us to never tell we were not paddled. Her subject was art, and she selected my flower along with Eddie Friend's to be shown in the county art show. After the show, she had bought us ice cream cones. It was a wonderful night. My fourth grade teacher, Miss Bailey, was memorable because she would finish each class with a story—the best being "Sabertooth the Tiger."

Miss Bailey's sister, the seventh grade art teacher, continued the storytelling tradition. In the fifth grade Miss Hildabrand taught me West Virginia history. I was mystified in the sixth grade when

Miss Lynch changed her name halfway through the year to Mrs. Fetty. My junior high career was punctuated with the most "D's" ever recorded as far as I know for three years at Morgantown Junior High. I even received a "D" in shop, much to the befuddlement of my carpenter father.

My academic career was nearing rock bottom. I had to plead with Miss Lambert, my 10th grade biology teacher, to give me a passing grade so that I might play basketball. It was all for naught. As a senior, I was dismissed from the basketball team after six games for general lack of interest and dislike of the coach. I was later forced into the humiliation of having to beg for a spot on the baseball team during my senior year in order to graduate from high school. The problem was the basketball coach was also the baseball coach. Back then you received academic credit for playing a sport. I needed the baseball credit after I meekly surrendered and departed my third year algebra class in the middle of a test. I then had to sit in study hall for two straight periods before heading off to driver's training taught by the football coach, whom I had tried to avoid after my undistinguished freshman year of football. I had been so successful at evading him that by my senior year—most memorable for having six different English teachers—he had no idea who I was.

Upon graduating high school, I struck out with a friend for the Atlantic City, New Jersey boardwalk to earn money for college. My real plan was to save enough money to buy two sweaters like the ones I saw a singer named Fabian wear on the television show *American Bandstand*. I had read that *American Bandstand* was going to be in Atlantic City and had some bizarre notion they would probably sell the Fabian sweaters there. Sure enough, I found them! The sweaters, one white, one tan, were long-sleeved with four buttons, and a rolled collar. They looked exactly like the ones Fabian wore. I bought them, paying them off during the six weeks I worked at the Flaming Angus Steak House ("only $1.19") in Atlantic City. My delight came when back in my hometown the sweaters were noticed. I felt special because it wasn't me wearing the sweaters. It was someone else, someone who was more—more everything—more like the famous teen singing sensation Fabian. I had been a tad self-conscious about wearing the sweaters, for a

Me wearing a "Fabian sweater."

couple of guys did laugh and call me "Fabian." Despite their laughter, I was pleased that the sweaters had garnered me the desired attention.

The Fabian sweaters could not, however, cover up my lack of knowledge nor camouflage a bushel-load of insecurity. I managed to secure a place at West Virginia University, but had no real commitment to becoming anything, being too busy dreaming, as if I were outside myself watching all around me. I knew early on even though my roots were strong that my life, unlike my parent's lives, would not be in Morgantown. Indeed it seemed as though I had already left and was merely playing out the cards until I really could leave. Perhaps my fantasy world was part of the process of finding myself. In looking back, I don't have a feeling for who I was, no real image of a true self, just a kid who must have seemed to be in a state of continual preoccupation.

Being so ill-prepared for college meant that I was doomed to take "bonehead" English. It took me several times to pass. I still have my grade report of having finally passed the English Proficiency test. I was honored to give the Commencement Address for the class of 2004 at West Virginia University where I spoke of my bonehead English travails. My 9th grade English teacher, Miss Burchnal, who is now a young 95 years of age, recently called me upon reading of my "bonehead" plight in college. She expressed concern that she had not done a good job of preparing me. I assured her that she had been in no way responsible for my ineptitude. It had been my responsibility, and I wanted full credit!

While I was truly a West Virginian, I was, in retrospect, a long way from the country and a longer way still from a coal tipple. My mother saw to that. She wanted me to run as hard and fast as I could to the other side of the mountain, but only after she made sure my shirt and pants were cleaned and pressed. My hair was always clean and combed. My body was sparkling clean. I had worked very hard on my accent. I had been told if I didn't want to sound like a hick and wanted to have a remote chance for a career in the theatre, I had better learn how to talk. The tongue of the hills was derived from European ancestors. But there were supposedly pockets in England where the hill dialect was quite similar, as though it was some ancient form of communication. This pattern

A BETTER PLACE

Graduation day.

of talk could be heard throughout Kentucky, Tennessee, Southern Illinois, and into the Ozark Mountains. My hillbilly lingo, I would stubbornly point out to my critics, was the Queen's English.

I felt a certain melancholy for West Virginia because it gave so much to my mother and father and because they gave so much to it. It nurtured a skinny, ignorant, insecure kid full of self-doubts who tended to daydream. Though I was unaware, West Virginia had seeped into my pores, into the marrow, and all the education in the world wasn't going to alter that. Education and travel and life did affect, I guess, my ability to blend in on my trips home, to talk as I once had, to see things as I once did, but there is an intimate knowledge and emotional attachment that is hard to ignore. Nostalgia can get in the way of ever being able to let go, but then there is no real need or want to.

10

MOTHER

My mother had a quiet grace and didn't know how beautiful she was. She was very reserved, yet she was what a West Virginian was about. Mom was why the world moved, especially my world. She was raised dirt poor in a coal camp in Brady, West Virginia, and was the oldest of six children, all of whom drank coffee because there was no pasteurized milk. Her Scottish coal miner dad and Hungarian mother came to West Virginia from southern Pennsylvania, having been recruited by Edna Gas and Coal Company. My grandfather Pete, a leprechaun of a man born in Monessen, Pennsylvania, had seen a better future when King Coal beckoned. He came into West Virginia to dig coal on his knees far underground for less than $15 a week. In the end, his body was bent and ravaged from years of crawling on his knees in mine shaft water and swallowing coal dust. His hands were so grotesquely crippled from arthritis, knuckles big as giant marbles, that he couldn't grip his coffee cup. The mines killed him. But he was proud and honored to be a coal miner, to be able to make a living for his family. He loved being a mountaineer. His eyes still had a glint behind his wire-rimmed glasses, and he loved teasing Grandma, "Can't do anything with her; she won't listen to a word I tell her. What am I gonna do with her?"

Grandma Elizabeth was born in Somerset, Pennsylvania. Her parents had immigrated to this country from Hungary and Grandpap Pete's from Scotland. Grandma's mother later ran off to Colorado with a miner, taking Grandma's younger sister and brother with her, leaving Grandma and her two other brothers behind. My great-grandmother died not long afterwards, leaving the two children she had taken, who had been put on a work farm, to struggle for survival. In later years they reconnected with my grandmother and their brothers.

My mother's parents were two of the many new faces in West Virginia during the period of 1910-1930. They had, I think, a much tougher road than my Dad's parents. Dad's birthplace on the farm was as clean and open and almost casual in its living as Mom's birthplace in the coal camp was hard, dirty and closed. On the farm, poverty wasn't visible, whereas it permeated the coal camp. The conditions in the mines were hellish, and hundreds of miners were killed accidentally or died a slow death from the bad air. Brady and Scott's Run were among the worst camps in the country.

Even as a child in the fifties who didn't know prosperity, when we traveled the ten miles to Grandma's house—an always freshly painted with green trim, clean-as-a-pin house in Everttsville—I stepped back in time. It was a way of life that was not easy or pretty except for Grandma's house with the white-painted stones that led to the outhouse. Grandma's house stood out from all the other mostly three and four room rough-boarded, drafty unpainted houses on the oil-caked road. I knew then that I was lucky to have grandparents who had struggled through and survived the desperate conditions of the coal camps.

Bad housing and the worst of slavery conditions persisted until code came in. But still the mines were punishing. My Uncle Junior's legs, having been smashed between two coal barges, are rubber, leaving him on crutches. His body is bent nearly in half, and he is only able to carry on because of a daily thirty-pill regime. My uncle Earl Ford long ago wheezed his last breath, his middle-aged body thin as a locust rail, his buzzard-hollowed face grinning through his wheezing and gasping for air because of black lung from the mines. This was the same for my Uncle Bub who spent his last years in a wheelchair tied to an oxygen tank. These men all maintained a sense of humor, optimism, hope, and a care for each other, especially when they were working. They had no illusions about equality when it came to social, political, and economic rights.

On my Dad's side the farmland is still there, and my aunt and uncle and cousins, with their families, still live on the land. But the coal camp of my mother's family is long gone and those relatives are scattered. But from both families there was that sense of quiet humor that one develops in West Virginia. There was also a sense of innocent joy, because there was no other life beyond the immediate hills. The outside world never intruded except for the exploiters—albeit they were a big intrusion.

My mother's story, like so many in West Virginia, is a testament to courage, unending hard work, and the will to survive. Mom's will was indomitable. Americans go to work. That's what we seem to do best. We work longer hours than any other industrialized nation and get less vacation time. All of us—firemen, policemen, plumbers, gardeners, coal miners, carpenters, doctors, nurses, bookkeepers—are workers; and Mom was the best and fiercest of workers. There was not a lazy or slow bone in her body. In a country of hard workers, I have never known anyone who physically worked as hard as she. She would not be subdued and went through life as a non-stop worker bee who wasn't the stay-at-home mom of the fifties. But she managed to prepare every meal for us, and my father's every meal, except when he was in the Navy during World War II. Prior to her death, she had thoughtfully left some pre-prepared meals in the freezer because I believe she knew she was sick.

My mother loved her parents, siblings, and in-laws; but come hell or high water once she got out of the coal camp she wasn't going back. Mom wanted to work—like the many who worked in the World Trade Center, like the Latinos, like the thousands who came into the coal fields—she and they all wanted to make improvements, to provide a good life for themselves and their families. Mom learned how to make every hard-earned penny count. She improved life for her husband and children by leaps and bounds, but she could never do enough. There was a weight on her shoulders felt by many in West Virginia—a certain resignation about life—that no matter how fast and hard you run, it would never be enough.

Mom always had the highest hopes for her children. I knew I would never follow my mother's side of the family into the coal mines. Mom wanted something else for me, something better. It is debatable whether acting is a better profession; it is certainly not more honorable. To this day I have never set foot in a producing coal mine. This is a sacrilege for a West Virginian, sort of like

Mom and Dad in front of the Greenbrier Hotel. Mom was not comfortable at the famed hotel.

a Costa Rican who has never tasted coffee. Mom so convinced me otherwise that I've never even gone inside the exhibition coal mine that is a tourist attraction in Beckley, West Virginia. But with her hand at my back, I have carried that wanting and needing work to define who and what I was or what I thought I ought to be.

One of my mother's friends said Mom always looked as if she had stepped out from the pages of *Vogue* "in a beautiful navy suit and wearing high heeled navy and white shoes." Mom was not by any means what one might think of as a mountain woman, though she was every bit a West Virginian. She was, despite having little money, able to dress with quiet elegant style, usually with a touch of red. She was always well dressed, always on her feet, always looking great—like the beautiful nature of the hills of West Virginia. But it was hard to get Mom to accompany me anywhere without her saying, "Oh, you just go; I don't have anything to wear." Mother was always uncomfortable at being complimented.

"Oh it's just an old thing," she'd say about a pretty dress she was wearing.

I was once brought up short by a gentleman who said, "I paid you a compliment, David; all you have to do is say 'thank you.'" I sort of did a chicken-kicking shuffle with my chin on my chest and thought of Mom and West Virginia. Mom was forever like West Virginia, compulsively apologizing for her shortcomings as she saw them. The only one to apologize more than me was my mother. But there was absolutely nothing that was inferior about her. She could draw looks walking down Fifth Avenue in New York City.

My mother had the innate talent to do many things. She made a great life and accomplished so much; but she could never overcome certain insecurities. I think those insecurities had to do with being a woman in West Virginia and hearing over and over again how backward you are. Her insecurities had to do with place. I took up her cross, her bane, whether it was her insecurities about her education or her obsession for cleanliness or her need to apologize for everything, including her death. Time has always had its way with me as it did with her—ever mindful that the clock is ticking—I inherited her impatience. That was part of my mother's legacy. She also ingrained in me the need to not let people down, to constantly remind them that you are sorry for your inadequacies.

On a bright California morning, a matter-of-fact nurse told me over the phone that Mom was in a coma; but the nurse was hesitant to say anything more until I spoke with the doctor, who was not available. I arrived at the hospital some hours later from my cross-country flight near midnight on a blustery fall day that was blowing December in ahead of schedule. Mom loved autumn, the chill in the air, the colors, even Halloween. A night watchman kindly asked if there was anything he could get me. The nurse on call was also nice as he walked me to Mom's room. They left me with the feeling of doom. Entering the room, I found Mom only being kept alive by a machine pumping breath into her. I think it must have hurt. I wanted it to stop. The sound! She was through running. Let her go, please God. Instantly I wanted to rip the machine off her. She would have told me to go home, that I must have something better to do. As I stood over her inert body caressing her face and telling her over and over that I was there, that I loved her, I could hear her saying, "You didn't need to come back, you should have saved your money, David." She didn't want me or anyone else to see her this way. She was shoving me out the door after making sure my coat was on. That was her way of giving me her love. Don't dote over me; go and do what you have to do.

Contentment, except when she looked at her children, and prosperity had not smiled on Mom. As I sat with her, I replayed in my mind an episode of the BBC series *Faulty Towers* where Faulty, John Cleese, is trying to get a dead body out of his hotel without being seen. I was tempted to carry Mom out of there. But like so many times, I didn't really know what to do but let things run their course. I felt helpless, useless. I told my sleeping mother, "We are just going to have to see this through." I could only sit with mother saying over and over "I'm here, Mom, I'm here. I will sit here, Mom, with you and watch your death." There was nothing to do—it was like watching a head-on collision. I sat there detached, like the chair I was sitting in. I was not going to duck out and make conversation with the nurses, and I didn't have any Xanax. I wouldn't ignore Mom's dying, as much as she would have liked me to. "I know you have something else to do," I could hear her repeatedly saying. "No, Mom, it's midnight and we're trapped, and I am not prepared for this." This was a test I hadn't studied for. I always had a face to put on for difficult situations, but there was no face for this. I felt like I had run out of fear.

If there were anything I ever needed, Mom, like most mothers, would have died to provide it. If I started for a glass of water, Mom would beat me to the sink. "Sit down, Mom. I'll get it." "No, I'm up, I'll get it." It was a game we played. She always won. No one ever worked or cared for a home more than Mom, but she could have walked away without glancing back. And I'm sure that's how she walked into death. Mom went out on her terms, no fuss, and no bother. Mom didn't want anyone waiting on her. If she couldn't get her own glass of water, she would just go thirsty. Her face of death was still beautiful but did not reveal much. She rarely let her guard down. Mom had endured, but we would never know the cost. She never volunteered her story. She was someone who had started from nothing, worked like a slave, kept her head above water, and survived with grace. Sitting with Mom in her hospital room for a few hours was one of the most intimate times I had ever had with her.

Another time was when she was typing one of my college papers in her determined head-on way, which was remarkable because she couldn't type very well. But I couldn't type at all, so she spent all night typing away with me sitting beside her, encouraging her along. We laughed the whole time until I went off to class with my paper in hand and with such appreciation and love for my mother.

When you lose your mother, you are never more vulnerable. I miss her today more than ever. I know I must have held tight to her when Dad went off to World War II. A child clings to his mother to be reassured. Perhaps she was clinging to me just as tightly as I was to her. When I think of home, my thoughts are wound around my mother. Mothers are havens of sharing, caring and grace. I have wondered if I had ever given her reason not to burden me with stories of her life, but I think that, for whatever reasons, Mom felt that her life could not possibly be of interest to anyone, even her son.

Only a short time before her death did she acknowledge how difficult life was in the coal camp, where shoes and water were luxuries. She went to her grave, giving as I recall, only two brief glimpses into her youth. One was an off-handed remark about getting her brothers and sisters ready for school. As the oldest child, she was in charge of raising her five siblings. Sometimes by the time she got them off for school, she had missed her school bus and would have to walk. She revealed this to me about a year before her death; in response to something my father had said about how hard it was for her to get to school. But as usual she did not elaborate, and I did not inquire.

Another glimpse into my mother's youth came when I found a picture she had on the arm of a lazy-boy chair I was about to collapse in. It was Mom as a young girl in high school. When I asked her the circumstances of the picture, all she said was that it was a play she had been in and she thought I might like to know that. My further questions were met with a quiet shrug. Childhood was something that Mom escaped from. She had no desire to go back to that place and no desire or need to tell me of that place. I only realized long after I was gone from home why. She had never really had a childhood in the coal camp community of Brady, where getting by day to day was a struggle with a coal company that knew all the tricks and ways to cheat the miners.

The only money to be had was in the form of company scrip that let her family buy overpriced items at the company store. Everything had to come from the company store. I keep a $5 token of scrip that says "Payable in Merchandise Only." When I was a teenager, Tennessee Ernie Ford's recording of *John Henry* "owing his soul to the company store" was a song that hit home. My mother, who knew the limits of the company store and who would never risk singing loud enough for you to really hear her, would ever so softly move her lips and sing along with Mr. Ford's rendition of *John Henry*. As a child I didn't know John Henry was black, just as I didn't know and wasn't taught that African Americans played a pivotal role in the coal story in West Virginia.

Mom's mind must have been so full and alive with the past that nothing from her childhood was dead. She just didn't want to talk about it. She knew that she was going to have to work and scratch to have a life. She married a carpenter. There would be no unrealistic desire for the big house on the hill or for the Cadillac in the garage. For Mom and Dad, life wasn't the easy one I saw on TV. It was tenuous, week-to-week, saving every penny making sure my brother and I had everything we needed. Mother was the most determined person I have ever known. She insisted on doing everything herself. Her first words must have been, "I can do it." If only she had believed it. Mom would have loved to attend college, but at the time it was not an option. She went to work in a bakeshop out of high school. After the war, she went to work as a sales clerk for Montgomery Ward and then worked for many years as a bookkeeper for an office supply firm. But all the while, she was a homemaker. She was a worker, a mother, a wife, and a wage earner who continually short-changed herself. She was a devoted daughter who looked after and cared for her mother. I have never known anyone who was as ambitious.

Mom, like Dad, had no natural instinct for laughter. It had been suppressed too long and could not be reclaimed. She did have every instinct for putting her beautiful black-haired head

A BETTER PLACE

My mom on the far right, with her three sisters, L to R: Maxine, Becky and Betty.

down and working as hard as any person has ever worked to make a home. This is what she saw her mother and father do. The image of Mom is immediate; she is on her hands and knees passionately scrubbing and waxing the gold-stained oak floors of her home. Her daily routine was clean, clean, clean: from the minute she got out of bed till she laid her head back on the pillow. Included in her day was her 9 to 5 job. Then it was home to fix dinner, wash clothes and iron. Mom sanded, painted, varnished, scrubbed and waxed. There literally was not an inch of that house that did not feel her determined hand. She had that same quiet respect for the mountains and deplored the sight of trash that was dumped down many a mountainside. It was an insult to her senses as though the trash had been dumped in her yard. "How can anyone do that," she would wonder aloud.

Mom's smile was like a young doe in headlights. She had desperately wanted out of the coal camp, and she made it only to discover, I think, that she still didn't feel a sense of belonging. She was a quiet sufferer. She never told anyone if she wasn't feeling well. Nor would she admit to herself how bad she felt, because she hated going to the doctor. I don't recall telling her about my insignificant problems. We never had soul-searching, gut-wrenching talks. She never complained. Sitting in her hospital room and watching her and the machines hooked up to her, I knew there would be no miracle. You could shout all you wanted, but she was on the other side. My father would take any involuntary movement as a ledge to hang on to, but it was a machine that was keeping her going. When morning came they unplugged that machine, and I prayed that Mom had found rest. For as she said on occasion when I would tell her to sit down, "I'll have plenty of time to rest."

Only late in life did Mom stop to read a book or magazine. Home for her was rarely a place to just sit and relax. Those were luxuries she couldn't afford. Neither was smoking, though she tried a few times hiding out in the living room to learn, but she failed. The only outward pleasures she seemed to take besides her children were her fairly regular bridge games with a group of women friends. They played almost every month for nearly forty years. Though she always said she wasn't any good, she seemed to truly enjoy those times. I would always ask how she did, and she often said she'd won the "the booby prize." But occasionally she would say in prideful surprise, "I won."

Dad has a corner for his baseball and American Legion mementos, but otherwise the house was Mom's domain, where she expressed herself with her decorating. Dad had always deferred to Mom when it came to fixing up the house. She would pick the colors, the pictures, the furniture, the wallpaper—everything. Part of Mom's legacy, as it is for many West Virginian women, is her home, her homemaking. Yet housekeeping did not begin to define who she was. She simply felt that you could tell a lot about a person by the way they cared for the place they lived. Her energy could be daunting, but it was because of her that I had some feeling for home, what home could mean, its demands.

My mother's presence is so close that sometimes I catch myself saying something to her, and I realize how desperately and unselfishly she loved me. When the time came she opened the door to my future. It was her anxieties that I took with me, her ambition, her fears, her frustrating need for perfection, but mostly and thankfully, I took her love. Mom's problem was that she was always giving; she was uncomfortable at receiving. She deflected inquiries about herself quickly and quietly. Early on as a young mother, she had a hot temper that I feel came from the frustration of not being able to do the things she knew she was capable of doing. I know that there was someone inside her that couldn't get out.

You could see how hard Mom went at life in her eyes; they were always searching. She was ever a realist. She did not keep anything that she didn't see a need for. There were four family photo albums, wrapped in plastic wrap, with few photos of her. To the end she wouldn't give herself the credit for keeping a family together. She discredited everything she did, but no one worked harder at perfection, which meant she could never be satisfied. In identical notes she left for my brother and me, she wrote:

Dear David,

I know you and Craig will share equally in whatever is left and remain the best of friends and care for one another the way you always have. Just be yourself. You and Craig have a lovely family. You both have compassion and love for family and friends. I am so proud of you both. I am just sorry I didn't spend more time with you when you were growing up and sorry I ever paddled you. I have loved you both more than you will ever know.

Love, Mom

11

THE CARPENTER

Few of us as children are concerned with anything beyond our childhood boundaries. But children are always stretching, always wanting the car window down, wanting nothing between them and the wonderful beyond. My children, like all children, are expanding their worlds, but with a somewhat cautious eye. As for all children, my dad's world as a youth was what he could see, taste, touch, and smell. It was the woods, animals, barley and wheat, the sun and moon and stars. It was Dad's joy of different kinds of wood and their use in building his house that carried him to his life's work. Dad's early education and who he is are tied to the land where he grew up.

His knowledge of native trees—walnut, chestnut, oak, cherry, among so many others—he learned not from books, but from growing up with and climbing them as a child. I recall being in a house with him that was built and finished with many different woods, and the owner was aptly proud. He was testing Dad, asking him if he knew what kind of wood this wall or that wall was. Dad never missed a one. When we were picking out an urn for Mom's ashes, Dad appreciatively picked up a wooden urn admiring the richness of the cherry wood until he realized what he was holding. He dropped it like a hot coal, but it was into the cherry wooden urn that Mom's ashes went.

Carpentry was something Dad had worked toward, something he wanted to do. He had learned a craft, a craft that he would gratefully practice for the rest of his working life. I have watched Dad deftly handle several old chisels and saws among other prized tools, while explaining what each was for. He recently rhapsodized about a few walnut boards he has cherished and stored down in his garage, so appreciative of their simple beauty. He knows that they "would bring a good price." He treasures them as much as anything he has. I have thought about his life and his work being a natural progression. It seems that as an adult he didn't have to give up who he was. He made an honest living. That was his aspiration. He was a master carpenter and as such was his own master. And except perhaps for being his own master and living in his own comfortable house, he had more in common with a metal worker or a wood gatherer in Afghanistan than a bond seller in the Twin Towers.

Running his hand over a tool as a lover would over a beautiful body, Dad asks if I could use any of the tools that he now had no practical use for. "I don't know what to do with them," he says. I wished that I could carry on with his tools and make his beautiful music. I recalled for him my high school shop class on the lathe machine where it took me thirteen various shapes of wooden legs before I got four that were rounded somewhat similar for my stool. I will one day display some of Dad's tools as art objects because they will keep him present to me each time I walk by them. But mostly these tools need to be in a carpenter's hands, creative hands, calloused hands. There is such simple universal truth and beauty in a workman and his craft. Dad's life had been built on good things.

Dad found his way as a carpenter, though as a twelve-year-old he had aspired to be an aviator. He was still very immersed in the fate of those on the airplanes of 9-11 and was grasping for some reason as to why it happened. "That's not what airplanes are for! This shouldn't be so." Dad had written of his desire to be an aviator in 1928, the year Amelia Earhart flew the Atlantic, after reading about Lindbergh flying the same ocean in 1927. As an adult, Dad doesn't like flying. "Isn't that odd," he remarks to me. We have had such romantic images of the airplane. Gore Vidal writes: "Flight would make men near-angels, it was believed; and a peaceful world one."[1] I'm sure that was the hope of the Wright Brothers after Kitty Hawk. Like my father and most of my kin, I have always been afraid to fly but embarrassed to admit it. Dad now readily agrees with the old joke that if God meant man to fly he would have given him wings. I don't believe any of my aunts and uncles and very few of my cousins have ever flown. Flying is not a means of transportation for many West Virginians. We still view it with a good dose of skepticism. Most of us would prefer "Beam me up, Scotty."

A few weeks after 9-11, Dad had told me over the phone that he had something he wanted to show me when I came home. When I arrived one late afternoon from California, he was trying to locate an old school "report" of his that he wanted me to see. He seemed nervous, a timid nervousness as he searched for his old school reports. I was afraid something was wrong. But he seemed better when he found the reports he was anxious for me to see. He laid them on the dining table, which had new placemats that were on top of the old dirty ones. Mom would not have been pleased. I made a mental note to remedy that situation. I noticed three pairs of shoes by Dad's chair. That was another mother no-no.

Dad handed me the old faded green folder, telling me that it "was a project, a report, for our club." "My Trip To The Mountains" is the title of Dad's report. He wrote it as a youthful assignment for the Trail Blazers Club. The club's motto was "all for one and one for all." My father wrote his paper in 1932, quoted in full in the preface. The title page was written in the hand of my grandmother Dessie, who was the club leader, lists Dad's age as 16. Dad was rather shy in showing me a glimpse of his childhood. Like Mom, he had never talked about his childhood other than to tell me a few times how far he had to walk to school.

As I read, he watched intently, looking for a hint of my reaction, for a sense of approval. He had made a slight nearly inaudible remark about his report "being nothing" that sounded vaguely like something my mother would have said about something she might have written. After I finished, I told him that I liked it. It was poetic. I was very touched for this was the first time Dad had shared something that he had written. I appreciated the smile on his face for its fullness, its soft warmth. His smiles can have a sadness, a resignation about them as though he knows a smile is only temporary. While having a kind soul, Dad's sense of joy was not often expressed. I don't recall ever hearing him laugh much.

To this day I can't imagine a belly laugh coming out of my father. A hit or a good play by a baseball player would bring a

The author with his father, Clyde.

smile and an "atta boy" from my dad the coach. Perhaps Dad had been a lonely child who was happiest when he was walking the fields and woods on the farm. Dad's sense of fun was expressed in a quiet, closed, reflective yet mildly contented way; but his was not what you would call a sunny disposition. It has become much sunnier with age. But my ancestors did not survive by being easygoing or light-hearted. Their lives were too unpredictable, too much on the edge.

When I asked Dad if I could keep his report, he was pleased. "I thought you might want it," he warmly smiled. He seemed relieved as if he had taken a chance in letting me see it. It was the father-son reversal of roles. He was a young boy hesitant to show me his work. He was afraid the stern teacher would toss it aside, not read it. Perhaps he was self-conscious of a young farm boy's awkward writing, remembering a certain disapproving high school

English teacher. Dad blamed that teacher for not helping the "less privileged students who lived out in the country" and for his not being able to graduate. "She told me I had no business being in her class. I never went back to that school."

Feeling second class is something that still plagues some of West Virginia's rural children. Dad carried that grudge for seventy odd years. He recalled that this same teacher asked him years later, when he was an established carpenter, to work on her house. He refused, though he could have used the money. I let it pass that there is a certificate stating he was awarded his high school equivalency diploma after he returned from the war. That is something to feel good about, but Dad still carries resentment for the now shadowy teacher.

Dad's "report" on his hike to the mountains was nothing earth-shattering: a young farm boy writing simply but movingly about a boyhood camping trip up the mountain. Back in 1932, Dad had none of today's conveniences, but would he trade his childhood of being able to hike the mountains at liberty like his ancestors had done? For him and his friend, it was pretty easy to get away to a place that was far away from adults. Dad even drew a picture of the cabin that he and his friend built in the mountains. It looks like Lincoln's childhood cabin, with a window and a stone fireplace. It was for Dad, I think, a way of expanding his boundaries, exploring and establishing his place in the world, much like his ancestors, where his fantasies could roam freely, and he could express his individuality and feel safe and serene.

Dad's willingness and eagerness to open up his past was welcomed and appreciated. He had shared his youthful camping report with me, and my delight in it gave him courage right then and there to share another report he had done in the sixth grade on his 4-H Club. "Where did you find these?" I asked in amazement. Dad told me he had found his youthful writings at the farm. "Nothing else is left." He said this pointedly with more than a tinge of sadness and unresolved anger. Dad's childhood reports, I think, were his way of reaching out to me and back to Mom. "You keep them," he said of his reports, "give them to your children." I told him I would. But there is no way these reports can mean for my children what they mean to me—at least now. This small act of Dad giving his confidence to me was an act of love; it let both of us look to the future. It told us something new about ourselves.

Through his reports he was telling me that he too had been young once. He seemed anxious for me to have something of his childhood, his heritage. Dad was trying to get close, intimate with me, have a real conversation for one of the few times in our lives, tell me something about himself and his life. Prior to my going back to West Virginia after 9-11, looking for just what I wasn't sure, Dad and I had, like Mom and I, never had a heart to heart. Perhaps I had not taken enough time or been interested enough to really question Dad or Mom about their youth. Perhaps I was too concerned with my own life, too self-absorbed. Maybe they thought I wouldn't be interested. Maybe they were right. Parents have a tendency to not want to bore their children because they know children do not like to be bored. Even after Mom's death, there was no epiphany for Dad and me of what we meant to each other or of what Mom meant to us, although Dad had written a short letter to me just prior to Mom's death.

Dear Son

It is not often I try to write letters, not because I don't want to, but find it hard to express the things I want to say... You see we always knew we had two of the best young men any Mother or Dad could have and we love you both very much.

Dad

Dad and I have had no trouble expressing our strong relationship to the land that is West Virginia, but we have had a problem expressing feelings in our close personal relationships. We didn't say such things in my family, not because we didn't want to, but as Dad said, it was hard to express the things you wanted to say. Why is that? I have tried to do better. Dad and I both have, and now quite readily express our love for each other. We had no tradition of language, not a great deal of spoken language to listen to when growing up. There was no language–even for grief. Dad has since told me how lost he was after Mom's death.

I wrote a book of poems about my mother's last autumn as a way of coping, as a way of finding my way back home. I have not shared these poems with Dad yet. I'm not sure why. Intimacy has not come easy for us. I never yelled at my father, nor had I opened up emotionally with him. But after Mom's death and 9-11, as we spent more time with each other, there have been a couple of regretful moments when I have lost my temper with him, when something elusive from the past reared its head. But it was those very moments that broke the barrier of never really saying anything of substance to each other.

Mom's death meant home was going to have a different meaning for Dad, my brother, and me. Home for Dad is his worn, lazy-boy chair where he sits like a lonely guest in a bed and breakfast, except there is no innkeeper. The loss of Mom naturally created a huge void in Dad's life. "I get so lonely." Dad had no wish or need to express himself by changing anything in the house since Mom died. The memories he and Mom shared have sustained him. Mom was like many other West Virginia women who spoiled their men. She did everything for Dad, and he was not prepared to cope with paying bills, washing clothes, and fixing food. He refused to learn how the washing machine worked. He would eat, but the food had to be put in front of him.

A few months after Mom's death, it was apparent that Dad needed help with the house and with himself. I arranged for Meals on Wheels to come to his house. "Who eats this stuff anyway? It sure doesn't taste like Sarah's," he complained. One day while doing a little yard work for him, suddenly one of the "meals on wheels" came flying over my head. "It's for the birds," he says. "Even they don't like 'em." There was that West Virginia sense of independence, I think, that also made it hard for Dad to accept those Meals on Wheels.

Dad understandably was having a tough time admitting that he needed help around the house. "How much will this cost me?"— The first question most West Virginians ask. I made him feel guilty by telling him that Mom would not want the house to be dirty. Dad greeted the first helper as though she were a telemarketer. Actually he is kind to telemarketers and buys everything they hustle, but he made it quite evident to the first victim that he wasn't comfortable with her presence. He felt invaded with someone traipsing around in Mom's house, handling Mom's things.

The next helper was the wife of a minister, an ex-truck driver who had founded his own church. The wife was rambunctious and seemed quite capable of handling an 18-wheeler herself. After a few weeks, Dad complained that she was "loud" and "she orders me around." West Virginia men don't like to be ordered around—especially by a woman, unless, of course, that woman is their wife. "All she does is talk, talk, talk, talk," Dad would complain. The minister's wife would tell me Dad was rude but said, "I try not to pay attention to him. I know he doesn't mean it." Dad would say, "Oh yes I do!" She told me that her husband had visited Dad and offered to pray with him, but Dad refused. "I go to church. I pray there," he told me.

The woman had asked for a new radio tape player so that she could listen to music while she worked. Dad was incredulous but on my next visit, I took him to Wal-Mart, and we bought a music player. I convinced him that he could listen to all the tapes he had bought from public television and Reader's Digest. On one of my visits, I happened to walk in on one of their "disagreements." The helper was rather loud and brusque with Dad, so I bit the bullet and told her that it would be best if she didn't return. She was barely out the door when Dad asked me. "What am I going to do with that music player?"

In dire need for someone to replace the minister's wife, I suggested to Dad that maybe we could find a man to help out. Teasingly, I asked him if he ever did housework. "Your mother handled all that." Apparently men in West Virginia don't do housework or admit it if they do. Unable to find someone to help, my brother and I took him out to a retirement home with extended care facilities. The first person Dad saw was on a walker. "Did you see that?" "Yes," I said. "She's old." "What are you?" "I'm not on one of those things." We looked at the dining room. There was a menu. "Nothing there I'd eat. Wouldn't be as good as Sarah's, or Bob's anyway." He was referring to Bob Evans, the restaurant.

Divinely, someone from Dad's Methodist church recommended the minister's daughter to me. The minister had performed a perfunctory service for Mom's funeral, and Dad seemed to like him at the time, but in a short order things went so bad with the minister's daughter that Dad reported that the minister wasn't speaking to him. Dad said he holds the minister no ill will. "If he doesn't want to speak to me that's all right, no great loss. I know better men. He's leaving anyway. Glad to see him go. Never done anything to him, but pay him." I did laugh.

Like most children, when Dad and his friend had the idea of building their cabin in the mountains, they instinctively wanted a secret place where they could commune with nature. We all wish for secret places. Dad, like a lot of West Virginians is trying to get back there to that place, to recapture the feeling of his youthful time on the mountain. For the moment he was able to see past what he rued and to acknowledge that the world has changed. My father is struggling to keep his world intact, as we all are. There are so many voids today. There is no longer "there" there, and it frustrates him, as it does all of us. The past has passed. The flower Mom planted right before she died is gone. The birds are different, and the neighbors are new.

It was the familiar world of Dad's childhood cabin that he yearned for. 9-11 had deepened my father's fear and suspicion; he had voiced a general distrust of things and people long before that. Perhaps the times of his youth—the Depression and WWII—had confronted him with a world where he met dishonesty, greed, guile, and suffering. Certainly he could have run into these things in West Virginia. In the wake of September 11th, he could only shake his head with confusion and sorrow when he would see a child with a gun, and that child was not going squirrel hunting, but was being tutored for war. Dad was increasingly emotional and resigned. Skyscrapers are as alien to him as they are perhaps to those who profess to hate us, those who wanted to see the skyscrapers scattered as dust to the wind. It is as Van Wyck Brooks wrote of man,

> *The vastness of modern cities, the mountain like buildings, the radio, the newspaper headlines perpetually changing create a mass-mindedness in him that reduces to nothing his sense of himself in a world to which he might otherwise have felt he belonged.*[2]

This is what some Muslims fear.

Dad hasn't read Thoreau, but Thoreau and Dad are of the same spirit when it comes to nature. Dad has always found pleasure in nature, and is most comfortable when he is surrounded by it, when it takes him back in time. He was amazed that there were fat and happy squirrels on my city land in Los Angeles along with deer and coyotes. Thoreau would have approved of Dad and his friend's childhood adventure, of their carrying supplies in a small cart and of experiencing nothing but the pleasures and green of the mountains with nothing between them and the stars. But Dad is resigned that today things are different.

Dad's homeland has an unspoken, unwritten history that was passed down into him, and he has carried that history in his bones, shyly and quietly but surely and proudly. He was exposed to and shaped by the environment, the remote hills that surrounded him as a child, by the land that he pressed with his feet and that had been trampled by his ancestors. He wonders about the future for the young. Today it seems increasingly difficult for young hill children to hike the mountain and build their cabin.

On Dad's youthful camping trip to the mountains, he, like his ancestors, recognized a good piece of land when he saw it. And today he hates to see it soiled by the cookie cutter houses that he sees springing up seemingly overnight. "Why do they build these things?" Dad's disgust is palpable. It's as if he has lost part of his freedom when he sees the houses on his old hiking trails. Perhaps freedom is the wrong word. Dad has not explored much more of this place than what he did as a child when he took his hike to the mountain, much like Thoreau who only got into real wilderness a few times. Dad's love for these mountains after reaching adulthood was, I suppose, just in knowing that they were there. He never went hiking or camping. He did walk the farmland, but he never took me to the mountains or told me about them or about his boyhood cabin when I was growing up.

Mountains are taken for granted by many West Virginians, but like a long-suffered hurt, mountains become part of you, part of your body, whether you felt them or climbed them or hunted them. Dad has never felt at ease anywhere but West Virginia. Sanctuary, I think, is what Dad believes is being compromised. That's what many West Virginians feel when they can't walk a mountain anymore because it has been fenced off, having been sold to a coal company. One of my childhood friends has put in a very up-scale housing development with an entry gate that my father-in-law, liking grand entrances, would have been proud of. The development sits high on land once owned by my Dad's mother's family overlooking the Cheat River and is near where Dad and his friend built their cabin so many years ago.

There is no zoning in West Virginia. Zoning, like seat belts and anti-gun talk, goes against the mountaineer's stubborn independent streak. One never knows if a gas station might pop up next door to your new house, so gated or closed communities can be the price for a certain kind of independence. West Virginia has generally not regulated the subdivision and development of land.

Though West Virginia seems on some days like a lost island where time has graciously stood still, the delay in total immersion of modernity is inevitable. The infringement into what was once "country" is something to be concerned about, especially when there is not a lot of thought given to the result. We are all in danger of creeping concrete. Perhaps it's just my sense of taste, but it seems the old houses have more character. When we moved into suburbia, Dad's house was the only "new" house in the neighborhood and is still one of a handful of "new houses." I call these houses by their old family names, even though the families have been gone for years. I still expect to see those faces, as they are very much present for me when Dad and I drive my old paper route.

One of Dad's favorite restaurants, Bob Evans—the other is called Apple Aunties—happens to be located in one of those commercial developments that look alike from state to state. This commercial park sits across Interstate 68 and is a stone's throw from the farmhouse Dad grew up in. When it was built, this interstate sliced right through the farm, cutting some of it away and landlocking about 22 acres that cannot be reached today because it's hemmed in between the interstate and the local airport. This loss of land use was without compensation from the state. So the birds and animals enjoy it free of encroachment by man.

Just recently Dad and his brother sold the landlocked land to a speculator who, I suppose, is hoping that the airport will expand one day and he will make a bundle. "Progress" has not moved as slowly as I thought in these parts. The shopping malls don't seem to bother Dad as much as they do me. Our malls, highways, and interchanges give us such a cookie cutter maze of concrete and overpasses that on a typical morning, I don't know whether I am entering Houston or leaving Indianapolis. West Virginia, like other states, is fighting for its soul. It's said that regional differences don't matter anymore. I tell Dad that West Virginia is different. He nods agreement. Of course Wal-Marts in West Virginia are like college students in Boston, too numerous to count. And t-shirts blazing the same advertisements are standard wear all over the country, including West Virginia. But Dad likes the mall. He can't get over the abundance of merchandise as we amble about in Lowe's, a store where everything and more for the home can be bought. "I've never seen anything like this," he says with a child's glow on Christmas morning. Indeed we are both rather amazed at all the "things."

One of the things Dad found the superstores sold were books. He raved about the novel *Seabiscuit*. This is the first book I ever recall him reading. He told me how he had read the book all day long and late into the night, and then he got up the next morning and finished it. "What a story. It was great. Have you read it?" I was speechless and had to confess I hadn't. Never had we come close to discussing a book before, and now Dad was ready for a literary discourse and I hadn't read the book! Dad had found freedom at the ripe old age of 88, and his freedom was in language. I can't remember seeing him so excited. Dad was right about the high school English teacher who sold him short and was responsible for his not being able to graduate with his class. How many West Virginians have been sold short? West Virginia ranks near the bottom for average number of books checked out of libraries per capita. Perhaps like Dad they have come to love Books A Million, a large bookstore chain. "You've never seen so many books," Dad exudes. "You can go in and sit down and read."

One day Dad asked me if I wanted to see Mom. I said yes, though I wasn't sure what he meant, Mom having been cremated. It turned out that Dad had a cement box built, and he put the cherry urn with Mom's ashes in a cement box and buried it with a gravestone in the Pleasant Hill Cemetery, a short distance from the farm where many of Dad's ancestors are buried, including an older brother who died quite young, a sister, and his mother and father. Mom could have cared less, but cemeteries are for the living, and it gave Dad some solace. Dad gave me a tour of all the gravestones, stopping at each one and recollecting what his memory would allow. We walked about the stones, grouped by family. The graves are rather nicely haphazard in their placement, but then the lives were pretty haphazard. "The names are on the stones. Otherwise I wouldn't know who's who. It's nice up here," Dad said taking in the view. "Good view," he continued. "Course I guess no one here's lookin' at the view. I'd like to see the view." I told Dad he could do what "Sit-up Wilson" did, who wanted to be buried sitting up so he could see the hills. So he left money and instructions that they build him an L-shaped cement tomb and set him in it so he could look at his beloved hills.

We stood in silence over Mom's gravestone. This is what it comes down to for all of us—one way or the other. It is the final spot, the immovable place. As we walked toward the car, Dad paused and motioned to a bare plot. "There's a spot here for you." I smiled and thanked him, but gently told him my home is with my family. He says he knows that, but wanted me to know there's always a place here "just in case." I smiled knowing that Dad always knew where he was going to be buried since he was a child, while I don't have a clue; and that as they say, makes all the difference. I know my place resides with my wife, my children, and that is where I shall be.

Back at the house, I asked Dad if he would show me his baseball clippings and pictures. He quickly led the way downstairs into the basement that he and Mom had converted into the civility of a "family room." I remembered helping to dig down a couple of feet so that the ceiling would be high enough. The furnishings include a pine wooden bureau that came from my mother's mother and a small oak desk that Dad had rescued somewhere and repaired and refinished. They are handsome and simple functional pieces. Dad's other salvages of his past include his family's old wall phone that had to be cranked up and a spinning wheel that

Dad's grandmother used. He ran his hand across the oak desk with a smooth caress. "Take them home with you," he eagerly said with a generosity that was touching. There is nothing he would like better than for me to take whatever I want, especially if he had made it or refinished it or used it.

He and I pored over pictures and articles that Mom had saved of his baseball teams. Dad and I tried to see how many players we could remember on the little league team he coached. "I don't believe any of these boys stayed around here. They never come back to their hometown." I come back, I told him.

Dad coached 35 years of American Legion baseball. Dad's teams did not lose many games. They won several state championships. In fact his team was playing a championship game in Mullens, West Virginia, the day I got married and my brother was pitching. My wife and I had attended the semi-finals. My brother was supposed to be my best man in the wedding but Dad wanted him to pitch the championship game, and that's what he did. Dad served as my best man. The team could do without the manager, but it couldn't do without its star pitcher. They won the game. I didn't question this decision because I knew the priorities; but my bride was not as accepting and has not let my brother forget. Though she is lighthearted with her reminders, she remains perplexed by my family.

Dad looked at the picture of that championship, commenting that the town of Mullens had had a rough time lately. Indeed the town was struggling to recover from the ravages of a "once in a hundred years flood"—there were several floods that year—that some say was a result of mountaintop mining removal that left nothing on the hills to hold the water back. Mullens lost nearly all its businesses, including the one-time hospital that my father-in-law had built. Looking at another baseball picture reminded Dad, "That boy couldn't hit a lick. I told his father he needed glasses. He threw a fit, said his boy didn't need glasses." Dad said he took the boy off the team, and then the father really went berserk. "I couldn't field a player who couldn't see. Would you?" Regarding Dad's challenging tone of voice, I shook my head, not daring to disagree. "The boy got glasses, and he still couldn't hit."

Looking over the baseball pictures brought back memories of

Mom and Dad working together to build Morgantown's first Little League baseball field. It is still used today and looks pretty much the same. "I remember Mom cutting the outfield grass. You and Mom created that field, you left your mark there." Dad shook his head, "It will go one day." "We'll all go," I said, "but someone will know you were here. You dug the field, you planted the grass." The makings of a communal home were in that baseball field.

Later, Dad and I went upstairs and sat down on an old blanket chest that he had also found somewhere and repaired and refinished. This was his first trip upstairs that I was aware of since Mom had died. Dad has not touched one thing of Mom's, not her soap, hair spray, lipstick or fingernail polish. Mom's clothes still hang in her closet. The odor of her life is in the house. For Dad, Mom is just upstairs making the beds and running the sweeper. The only reason he would consider moving is if he could build his boyhood cabin again on the land of his childhood. He knows he won't, but is hopeful that either my brother or I will.

We looked at a few family pictures together that we had not seen in years. There was a photo of Dad as a dashing sailor in his uniform with the white striped flap on the back. After looking at a couple of other Navy shots, Dad opened the chest we were sitting on, and there along with my college "beanie" was his Navy cap. One of my favorite pictures is of me as a young boy in my grandmother's arms with Dad's Navy cap on my head. I asked, "Does it still fit?" He fondled his old cap and then asked me; "What will you do with the house?" I told him there was plenty of time to worry about the house. "I wouldn't say there's plenty of time, I hope but…I could kick the bucket." His voice trailed off. I assured him not to worry but I was non-committal.

When my father passes on, if I am still around and my brother agrees, I will not let the house stand empty. Joyce Carol Oates comments, "The house contains the home but is not identical with it. The house anticipates the home and will likely survive it, reverting again simply to house when home (that is, life) departs. For only where there is life can there be home."[3] In time Mom and Dad's house will be made a home by another family. It is a house that, if treated with just some of the care my parents gave it, will provide shelter and be a place where others' memories will be rich and their lives close and as ordinary as ours were. If the house is cared for, it will remain a place for the possibility of home. But if somewhere down the line it falls into disrepair and disuse and finally abandonment, then what Joyce Carol Oates says will be true for Mom and Dad's house, "...there has been a sad story."

Dad, his head down on his chest and his hands folded in his lap, says, "I know your life is not here." Home has meant something to Dad that he has never gotten away from, never wanted to get away from. He has never needed or wished to expand his meaning of home. "I like it here; it's a good place to live." I tell him that I like it there, too. "Do you think you'd ever move back?" Over the years, I have entertained the idea of moving back to West Virginia. I explained that my wife and I want to be where our children live and that is in California. I wonder again when Dad asks about his grandchildren, how they are and what they do, if I have worked hard enough to keep our families close—feeling that if I have not done my part, I have let down a part of home. Perhaps it was the thinking of my parents and myself that home was the house I grew up in, the town where I was raised, and thus it was my obligation to return with my family.

Knowing members of one's family takes time and commitment and trust and a willingness to risk hurt and today—more than ever—a willingness to travel. My parents, especially Dad, as others from their time and place, were not comfortable with the mobile movement of my generation, a movement that ironically had been given its birth with the end of World War II. That opened up places never before dreamed of, possibilities for ordinary people. So many West Virginia parents today of necessity are bidding their children farewell, resigning themselves to watching their children from afar as the children forge paths toward an out of state home. It will take a concerted effort to keep the family bonds. A house can become an island that becomes increasingly remote for the children who move on, children who have expanded horizons with new ideas, who have a different, perhaps more encompassing view of democracy. This is a crucial period for West Virginia because with the large numbers of young people leaving the state, it puts in jeopardy the very thing that is vital to West Virginia's way of life, and that is family.

Dad and I sat silently for a time with no words passing, and then reminisced over a few more photos. This sitting beside each other with the book of photos spread across our laps was as close as son and father would get. It was an easy relationship. My confidence soared. We were like two brothers laughing, and trading stories, something out of character for us. We sat there so easily looking at the pictures letting them take us back, back all the way. This was a new experience for both of us. Dad stared a long time at a photo of Mom. It is one of the few photos of her. "Sarah was hard to figure," he finally says. He has told me a number of times that he gave Mom whatever she wanted. "If she needed a dollar, I gave it to her. When she was sick, she told me, 'Thank you for building me our house.'" Dad said this with some energy. Did his tone have a bit of self-congratulating? No, he was just telling me in his way how much he loved Mom. I think it's a very male thing to enjoy providing for loved ones. "She loved this house, Dad," I assured him. "You did good." I patted his back. "Not bad for a country boy," he replied.

Dad has often reminded me of how he "worked like the devil for every penny I ever had. Nobody ever gave me a thing." He rued the times he never had "a dime to shine," or "two pennies to rub together," "didn't have a nickel to my name." Dad was ever waiting for word that he had won either or both the Publisher's Clearing House Sweepstakes or the *Reader's Digest* Sweepstakes. At first I didn't see any harm. I had always been convinced that I would win. I filled out every sweepstakes that the mailman delivered. "Someone had to win. Why not us, Dad?" He kept buying more and more magazines though, more books, and tapes—because he was convinced that he was going to win. He believed a woman from *Time* Magazine was sending him personal letters suggesting that she would "make sure he would win something." Dad said that he had talked personally to a man at *Reader's Digest*. "He told me I had an excellent chance of winning. Eight hundred thousand dollars! A farm boy like me who never had anything, how about that?"

"Maybe entering these sweepstakes should be part of West Virginian's economic development plan," I joked. Dad says, "Maybe they are." "If you win," I told him, "they'll put your picture in the paper, and everyone will know where to come for money." Dad thought about that for a moment. "People would be all over me—like that fellow who won the lottery. Someone hit him over the head and robbed him." Dad worried a little. "Can you believe that? I'll just have to hide out. They said I would have a car, too. I don't know what I'm going to do with the car. Guess I'll just park it."

He was absolutely convinced that he was going to win. There was no way to persuade him otherwise. It was a big lie, a scam, fraud, that I had helped perpetuate. It took Dad a full year to get over his deep disappointment of not winning. There is no corporate social conscience. The only goal is to make money—sell, sell, sell. My brother had called *Reader's Digest* and asked them to stop sending material to Dad. A few months later, I received a gift subscription from Dad to *Reader's Digest*. In January 2004, I received yet another gift subscription from *Reader's Digest*, again courtesy of Dad.

Dad moved his eyes around the room, seeing every nail he drove. "It was a good place to live," he says. "Yes, Dad it was and is," I assure him. "Like West Virginia," he says. I laughed and agreed. When finished looking at the photos he said, "I'm glad we did that." I looked at him and smiled, and told him the pleasure I was having in those moments with him. Dad had left a trail, footsteps. He wanted to make sure I saw them. He wanted me to know how he felt about things, how he feels about West Virginia, how he appreciates its beauty, and how he left his homeland, the beloved farm where he was born, to make his way in life. West Virginia, like Dad, is trying hard to hang onto its heritage, its center of tradition, its memory of what it once aspired to be so that there will not be a sad story. Dad had been a child with dreams, a memory, and now he seems to be looking back for those who are long gone to talk to him, guide him.

"I get lonely if I think too much. So I don't think. I'm all right though." But still Dad combs the underbrush, looking for some lost rooted fence post that he set as a young boy or a certain rock that he is sure "is here somewhere." He knows what he's thinking of, he can see it, and that's the important thing. He wants me to see it, to feel it, to know how it was for him, so I search with him, for him and for myself, for a safe passage of what has gone before.

When I told Dad I read that the weather had been unseasonably warm in West Virginia, he said that "the last four or five days had been something. The sky was such a deep blue it hurt my eyes. I fell in love with West Virginia for the second time." Perhaps he has even more in common with Thoreau than I thought. He said it like a lover to a woman, a woman who is so beautiful—like my mother—she would be hard to describe. But Dad found the words. That English teacher missed a diamond in the rough and could have learned something from the student she dismissed too quickly.

The sun does seems bluer cutting through a thick fog that lines the hollow floors and lingers, overstaying its welcome as Dad and I take the old family Sunday drive. We walked his land on a late afternoon under a cloudless sky. Again I was reminiscent of Thoreau:

We walked in so pure and bright a light, gilding the withered grass and leaves, so softly and serenely bright, I thought I had never bathed in such golden flood, without a ripple or a murmur to it. The west side of every wood and rising ground gleamed like the boundary of Elysium, and the sun on our backs seemed like a gentle herdsman driving us home at evening.[4]

Dad loves the seventeen acres of the original farm he has title to today. It gives him comfort to walk on his acres, to retrace his footsteps, and to think about those footsteps that came before his. In part, my father has held onto the past by way of the few acres that he inherited. He stops our walk to rest. He looks around and then looks directly at me and says, "When I come here, I feel as though I've come home. I just love it." His rest is short as he is determined for me to walk his land. He seemed to gain renewed energy. He was breathing heavily when we reached the top of a hill, but he delighted in pointing out to me the different kinds of trees and bushes. We climbed to a cleared, flat piece of land. Dad was nostalgic and somewhat sad as he pointed out an apple tree he and Mom had planted. He had wanted to build them a house there but "that won't happen now."

We made our way through the underbrush that had grown up after the acres had been logged several years back. "The s.o.b.," Dad said with palpable anger in his voice about the logger, "He cut trees he wasn't supposed to. I had marked what ones he could cut. You got to be right with them, or they'll rob you blind." The greedy logger did nothing that the coal and lumber companies haven't been doing to West Virginia and its people for years. Dad said, "It's a doggone shame. I told the man what he could cut. There was a forest here, trees....what's that one tree...God, I know it like I know my name." His memory now goes in and out like a cloud, frustrating him as he tries to connect the dots of his history.

Dad will try to remember a name or place or just something he wanted to tell me. He concentrates with his head in his hands trying to solve the puzzle. When the fog persists, when Dad can't come up with a specific, I try and guess what he is after. But at times it is hard to know what he is thinking, what he is seeing. Sometimes I can, sometimes I take a stab at what he's after, other times we simply go on. When he talks about trees and can't come up with a name, I usually shrug because I don't know trees the way he does. He says again with even more frustration, "I know that tree like I know my name," shaking his head and clenching his fist. "Why can't I think of it?" I have no answer nor really do his doctors. I try and console him and tell him it's no big deal if he forgets something every now and then, that I can't remember my own name half the time. He shakes his head saying, "Frustrating, isn't it?"

"It's embarrassing when I can't come up with a person's name and I've known that person for years. You feel like a fool. God I hate this. I could choke myself." He smiles but his face is almost a sad smile of quiet frustration. He says almost with a throw away tone, "That's just the way it is now, I guess. I don't have any complaints." "At least you still recognize them," I laugh trying to keep his sail aloft. I put my arm around his shoulder, a gesture that I had only recently gotten comfortable with. Dad tends to give me a hug now rather than just a handshake. It's an awkward mountain-man hug, sort of like two first-time puppy lovers. But while there is a little awkwardness in our hugs, there is also gratefulness, two men glad to see each other. A hug goes far.

Old memories and old ghosts dogged our every step as we eagerly retraced old footsteps plowing for nuggets of the past. But unearthing them takes me up and down and around the many hills and curves of Dad's mind. That he was now, nearly 90 years later, seeing and loving the place where he grew up, well, it was like meeting an old high school sweetheart and falling in love again. Perhaps I have not loved my homeland as much as my father. In post 9-11 and with the memory of Mom's death hovering, Dad and I, in walking his land, were seeking the continuity of family, a family that had never shown a big need for any tradition or for reasons to celebrate.

We go on, looking for a certain stone that he remembers as a marking for a boundary. His history is not lost; you can see it in his face. At times he is quite lucid on the details of his geography. It swirls around in his mind and bones and stops here and there with an echo of what once was. History permeates his being. Dad knows his land, the things that live on it, where the sun hits as it passes over, how the trees serve as a buffer from the wind for the flat piece of land where he had wanted to build, when the creek would run dry, how deep he would have to drill for water—so many vital things to know and understand about one's place. Dad pointed out all the different remaining trees. "There's still some good ones left. You could log them; there's a little money here." I told him to let them grow. Suddenly something ran through the brush and thick trees. "It's a deer, see it?" Dad suddenly smiled and I could picture him as a child. He showed me tracks and droppings. Despite Dad's rural upbringing or because of it, he had never, to my knowledge, been deer hunting. He couldn't shoot one if he were starving.

Seeing the deer energized Dad. He was home on his land and was a child once more talking to the trees and animals with no urge to harm. He wishes the trees could talk, that the old oak was really wise and strong enough to withstand man's assault. He was seeing a place that doesn't exist anymore. The farmhouse is still there as is some of the land, but progress is looming in sight across the hill as apartments are springing up. The farm is a short step from being the kind of development Dad rues. Despite my Dad's brother and his children and grandchildren staying on the farm, the prospects of them holding onto what's left of the farm do not look promising. Progress will tighten its grip; the pressure to sell will grow.

Life has been a daily grind in ways, leaving Dad to wonder, as we all do, where it went. He has to find a new path in all the underbrush that we trample. His old footsteps are buried. How quickly the future shrinks, gets dark. Dad's smile was closing down as fast as the late afternoon light. He is determinedly, and deservedly, set in his ways, thinking about the next life. We come to a barbed wire fence marking the end of his land. Dad can only hope that whoever ends up with the land will treat it gently. "Maybe you'll build a place here." He doesn't expect an answer. Of course, I think if the world goes to hell in a hand basket and we have not evaporated, I can always take my family to my Dad's land. We could build a cabin from the rocks and trees and plant a garden and start all over again. There is nothing Dad would like more, because I would be coming home.

He felt more than just sentimentality as he leaned against a fencepost that may have been set by his grandfather. Though Dad had moved off the farm as a young man, he had never really left. Now here he stood in the brush, his eyes seeming to take in everything on his land. For a moment he was escaping his solitary destiny, a destiny that was drawing him closer to the great mystery. I thought of this country and how it is still relatively young, but already has so much history behind it. I wondered how much was ahead. At that moment looking out at his acres from where he and Mom planted the apple tree, Dad smiled almost joyfully, and I thought he was close to his destiny. There was joy in his smile, and it was the joy of life. This joy is an enabler. "Thanks for coming out here," he said.

West Virginia's effect on me is still hard to describe, just as I can't find words for who or what I am—I am not good at those kind of questions. Perhaps the first time the blue sky hurt Dad's eyes, the first time he fell in love with West Virginia, was that trip to the mountains as a young boy to build his cabin. He considered this "the best place he had found." It was a fleeting but still remembered moment of poetry where he felt the rush of water cascade over him without hitting his head on the rocks.

There's been a long stretch of time, a lifetime, between his original vows of love for a place and the time he spent getting up and working like a dog, obediently following the routine of life, and the time now when he feels an ebbing of responsibility. But there is no ebbing of love for me, or his place, West Virginia.

12

A WEST VIRGINIA DOCTOR

My father-in-law, Dr. Ross Newman, was a doctor's doctor, a wonderful surgeon who was polite with unmatched bedside manners, earning his patients' love and respect. He received numerous honors, as well as assorted Christmas and birthday gifts every year. The kind doctor did not pay much attention to these tokens of appreciation. Gifts were never discarded, but the assorted gift bottles of liquor were stored in the attic of his house. The gifts of liquor piled up for years, for, like Lincoln, he never drank, not so much as a glass of beer. Like my mother, Ross was not comfortable receiving gifts. Like my mother, he was always the observer at Christmas sitting quietly off to the side delighting in what others received. He tolerated Christmas, like he tolerated any other holiday, as something to be endured.

He was a naturally gentle, headstrong, driven, rigid, somewhat vain, formal, native Virginian who was impressed with appearances. He was born not far from the West Virginia border, near Pulaski, Virginia. After viewing some pictures of his home and family, I realized that there were parts of southwest Virginia not unlike the poorest parts of West Virginia. Aristocracy and gentility did not necessarily commence at the Virginia border. Ross had been dirt poor growing up, something he rarely discussed.

My mother-in-law, Claudeis, said that her husband loved his parents, especially his mother. His father "was a bear" and was responsible for his son's difficult childhood. She said her husband had tried to pretend that nothing bad ever happened in his family. "To hear him talk you'd think it was *Life With Father*." That was what he wanted, what he dreamed of, but his desperation to get away from the impoverished childhood had consumed his best intentions. Like my mother, my father-in-law had a quiet stubborn desire to move beyond the life he was born into. They both shared a consuming determination and ambition that allowed them to reach for and attain a better life. What they achieved in life was a testament to their iron clad strength of will.

Even though Ross was born in Virginia, both he and my father had similar small farm backgrounds and similar dreams for their futures. My father-in-law was fifteen years older than my father and had gone to Randolph Macon College on a music scholarship. He got his medical degree from Louisiana State University Medical School. It had taken him a few extra years to complete his studies because he had to stop school periodically in order to work. Though he never traveled outside the country and despite his upbringing, he had a rather cosmopolitan air about him, probably as a result of his education.

My father-in-law's first job after his residency at Charity Hospital in Shreveport, Louisiana, was at a hospital in Beckley, West Virginia, in 1935 at the age of 34. He had followed his older sister, a nurse, to Beckley. She had told him of the need for surgeons in the hills—a need that is still there. The sister-in-law and her brother, my mother-in-law wrote, had been "glued at the hip. He confides in her before he'll tell me anything."

My mother-in-law, with a tone of resignation, complained about her husband's choice of locations. "He could have gone anywhere in the country, but he wanted to come up here." The doctor practiced medicine in West Virginia for the next fifty years. He built a hospital deep in Appalachia, where the need was great. He never turned a patient away. He set broken arms and treated skinned knees with the same care that he removed a tumor. My wife says her father was the most eccentric person she has ever known, while her mother, in stark contrast, was the most ordinary "normal" person she has ever known. The doctor never could resist trying to impress people.

Claudeis called people as she saw them. If you didn't have something to say, then you should keep quiet. She was a warm, shy, but no-nonsense woman who, despite her protestations, fit right in with those West Virginians who were not afraid to speak their minds.

My father-in-law toiled terribly hard to extricate himself from the past. He never stopped learning and had relentlessly high expectations for his children. Ross was perhaps the most focused person I ever knew. What he wasn't was a hick, a stereotype of somebody's assumption of what a man from Appalachia was like. There did not seem to be anything "country" in him. He was a very reserved and complicated, yet simple and civil man with whom I shared some fabulous laughs. Ross, like my mother, had no desire to return to his roots, no real ties to the land, not even for sentimental reasons, although he did have a desire to spruce up the homeplace, to dress it up a little and to perhaps let him forget what it had been. Making the homestead "presentable" was not for his father and mother but for himself. I found a letter written by my father-in-law to his father, saying that he was sending money home so that a picket fence could be built around his father's house.

In all the years I knew him the doctor rarely talked of home—despite being close to his four brothers and one sister. He helped them in any way he could—and also loaned his father money from time to time. He never spoke of his family, at least to me, and always kept things fairly formal with his brothers and even with his sister.

In contrast, Claudeis was always talking about family. She said of her mother, "She was always ready to bring me back in line however she could. She would send me after my stepfather in the bar and he would give me a piece of candy and tell me to go home." She delighted in talking about her past, in telling stories like when my wife as a child had put bubblegum in her stepfather's hair and it had to be cut out. Her stories were ways of coming to terms with her life. Her real father and a sister had died in 1918 of diphtheria, the same year I recently discovered that my Dad's slightly older brother had died with the same fever.

It was fascinating and a privilege to become part of a family that had ghosts in the attic. In my family there were no attics to rummage around in. When my in-laws passed on, they left their home and attic full of remnants of their lives for me to touch and smell and read. It made me think more about my own family's history and how West Virginia, that unique place, was imprinted on me. There was a lifetime collection of items in my in-laws'

My father-in-law, Dr. Ross Newman.

attic about my wife's—at first glance—golden past. There were numerous items that made my wife's past, her home and place, come alive for me. I was transfixed by what the trunks and boxes held. There were albums constituting a family's history. Among the items in the attic were scrapbooks, filled with my wife's growing up years through her college years, complete with notations. She had no recollection of these scrapbooks. You can imagine our surprise when we realized the notations were all written in her father's handwriting as though she had written them. Her father had painstakingly filled the scrapbooks with "keepsakes" from all her activities, including her school report cards. She got all "A's," which did not surprise her father or me.

Among our discoveries was a collection of my deceased father-in-law's love letters to his intended. The letters, written daily in a six-month period in 1935, were carefully bound with a pretty blue ribbon and were among a number of things that told me attics can be treasure troves of a surprising history. The letters were a revelation about my wife's father. In them he came across as a compassionate, jealous man who was deeply in love with the pretty young nurse he had left back in Louisiana. He was very intimate in his letters, the kind of intimacy that one didn't expect of him.

My wife knew her of father's love and passion for medicine. She had not seen his romantic side. He was in his letters as in life—steely determined. But this was countered with gentility and a sense of fun, reserved as it was, like my mother's. Even my wife, who could not understand why her parents had stayed married, came to see how her mother fell in love with her father. Of course his way of living, his strict code of how life should be lived, was such that a divorce would have been unthinkable.

In taking the job in West Virginia, the doctor was forced to do his courting via letters. His was trying to convince his sweetheart nurse to follow him to West Virginia. My wife's father wrote to his darling about the town of Beckley in 1935: "Things seem to be humming around here as though there had been no depression… it is a fairly prosperous little town…" This was in stark contrast to my mother's life in the coal camp and much of the life in West Virginia during the Depression. But my father-in-law was intent on painting a pretty picture for his bride-to-be. He sent her a number of postcards about this "beautiful place West Virginia." Another letter of my father-in-law's persuades, "Things are not dirty and smoky around here in Beckley at all. The coal here is smokeless coal—and the town and adjacent sections are clean… and the weather is just grand. I do not perspire any in comparison to that in Shreveport. The hospital is the most up-to-date and cleanest I've ever visited. The library is beautiful and the lawn in front is just marvelous. It's quiet and peaceful. No politics."

Maybe West Virginia politics paled in comparison to Huey Long's politics in Louisiana, but there was and to a large extent still is nothing but politics in West Virginia. Since my father-in-law wrote his letter, the tawdry acts by some of West Virginia's past governors might have brought a blush to even Huey Long's face. In another letter, my father-in-law opined about Long's assassination that he "was sorry to hear of his being shot like that. Would like to have seen him gotten out by popular vote and not shot to death to get out."

The notion that there were no politics in West Virginia shows the innocence of a man who was so desperately in love and would say anything to win his sweetheart, but it is also a man who had found the possibility of a life—of home. Expressing his love in his letters was risky because she may have not written back. In fact he was terribly upset when her letters were slow in arriving. He could see the importance of love, the possibilities of it. But his life would require the woman he loved to be subordinate to his desires, his ambition. She would have to relocate her life. In truth my mother-in-law's mother did not want her daughter to come north. The doctor was relentless in his pursuit. Finally, over her mother's objection, the doctor's sweetheart joined him. They were married and lived the rest of their years in Beckley. My mother-in-law never really took to the hills, though one of her favorite pastimes was voicing her strong opinions about West Virginia politics and politicians.

My father-in-law's letters were as good as a museum for letting us understand a bit of the 20th century, especially when it came to life and doctoring in the towns of Beckley and Mullens. One letter detailed the instantaneous transmission of a voice from London, England. Ross sat in the Memorial Building in Beckley listening to the voice and marveled that "the conversation was just as plain as if you were in the room with them, and questions and conversations immediate. No lapse at all for time in transit. The lights were switched off and a machine arranged a graphical picture of the conversation between the men in London and here. It was one of the most interesting things I have heard and seen in some time." He had gone straight back to his room and written about it to his sweetheart. Ross had written about his fear of the coming war in one of his letters: "What do you think of the war situation in Northwestern Africa? Don't believe U.S. will become involved but you never can tell. Of course I stand about the right kind to get the first call—but I think things will clear up by that time." He would have been 40 in 1941, and was not called. The hospital needed to keep some of their doctors. That and his age exempted him.

One of his letters detailed his distress over an elderly black man that was turned away at the hospital for lack of funds. Ross mentions that an O.B. case "gets about $125.00 to $150.00 for each private delivery. So you see they clean up in that sort of thing." He talks about the movies, about his travels through West Virginia, and of course he writes extensively about being a doctor, proudly noting in detail his operations and the procedures of the time. He mentions removing 16 tonsils in one day. "At the rate I am going, I will do well over 200 major operations my first year. I think that is pretty good, don't you sugar?" It was a portent of her future.

My father-in-law, in trying to escape his Appalachian roots, caused some resentment in his family by his need to show that he was a good provider. He had distinct ideas about the kind of house they would live in: it would be big, strong, and imposing. The doctor was trying desperately to create history, a sense of tradition, of ritual, something stable, solid, safe and yes, predictable. He wanted his children to feel things that he had never felt and couldn't feel. Nothing pleased him more than being able to give my wife and her brother whatever he thought they would want. There was nothing to be done, as my wife said, "Daddy was going to do want he wanted to do."

My first car by marriage was a '59 2-door red and white

My father-in-law and his Packard.

Oldsmobile. Ross had given it to my wife for her high school graduation. Ten years later we were living in New York City where the Olds was towed by the parking enforcers a couple of times. The second time, we asked what happens to towed cars that are not claimed. The answer was, "They're auctioned off." We couldn't imagine they got much for it. My father-in-law's next gift to us was a metallic gold two-door Pontiac. We were grateful because we needed a car at that time, as we were living in upstate New York.

One night in New York City, returning to the parking lot at 10th and 46th street after work, the Pontiac would not start. The parking attendant, whose name was Bob and whom I liked because he was nice and actually knew where West Virginia was, told me he knew someone who could resurrect the car. Bob was a trustful soul and a mountain man at heart whom my father-in-law, appreciating eccentricities, would have delighted in. Bob had bought a long shiny black stretch Cadillac limousine for his wife and mother-in-law. It sat beside the attendant's shed. He told me he had been saving for years to buy the limo. "I could chauffer you around West Virginia. They would think you were a big star."

A BETTER PLACE

My mother-in-law, Claudeis Newman.

Bob's wife and mother-in-law, whom everyone seemed to know, spent the evening hours in the limo watching television, rigged with a power cord from the shed where atop the roof was a small antenna leaning at a precarious angle. Bob said it probably reminded me of "the hillbilly with the Cadillac parked in front of his shack and the television antenna poking up off the tin roof." Bob's wife and mother-in-law cooked their meals in the shed on a hot plate and ate in the limo every evening on china and silver with cloth napkins. Bob, in a chauffeur's cap sat in the driver's seat and the women, so dignified in full make-up and well-dressed with jewelry and their coal black hair, sat in back. Bob told me they were from Romania. "We're gypsies," he confided. The women were always saving me a piece of desert and once invited me to a birthday dinner that Mamma Leone's was giving them at the then famous restaurant.

On one cold Christmas season night, my son and I took the Hudson train in from Pleasantville, New York, to Grand Central Station to pick up our "wheels." On a prior visit to see the progress of the patient, I had found the shell of the Pontiac parked on cement blocks with the wheels and engine gone, but Bob told me not to worry. As my son and I neared the parking lot magically there was the Pontiac wrapped with a red bow, and my son and I were greeted with "Here Comes Santa Claus." My son was too young to appreciate the significance of the song. There was a big oil drum with a fire going in it. My son and I gathered around the fire with Bob, his wife, and mother-in-law, the mechanic and assorted elves. We sang carols and listened to all the stories about the adventures in repairing the Pontiac.

It was a special Christmas night for my son and me, for it was a moment in time where a few people looked at one another in a new way and saw that we were all part of the same mountain, the same family. The price of the "resurrection" of the Pontiac was reasonable, and it ran perfectly for the next several years until my father-in-law gifted us yet again.

The third and last vehicle he bought us—right before we were moving to California—was the infamous silver Bronco, aptly named for it would throw you every time, especially when it sensed you depended on it the most. It became a source of frustration for me, several mechanics, and especially for my wife. My father-in-law had assured me "it's a fine, big, strong car, safe one, too, for your children." He was a one time proud Packard owner and liked big and strong and solid, whether it was luggage, houses, or cars.

I found it hard to look this gift horse in the mouth, especially when it came with such high recommendations. "Hi, Ho, Silver," the seller smiled. "It's a truck, Daddy," my daughter noted. It had tractor wheels. "This rig is just the ticket," the eager seller said—starting to circle the Bronco and stopping to punctuate his delivery with a good kick to each tire. "It used to belong to the sheriff. It's built like a horse, (kick) been all over these mountains chasin' shiners. It gets up in the hollows where a mule can't get. (kick) This baby's got good legs." (kick) And it's made in the USA!" (two kicks) That was my warranty, my "as is." He told me he had given me a good price. My father-in-law gave me a wink.

The seller apparently didn't know that my father-in-law was footing the bill. He issued a deep concerned warning: "Think of your children; you want them protected and safe, and it would give me such solace to know that their mother can drive her children around in such a forceful vehicle. You want to be careful because I've been having terrible premonitions." "Like what?" I queasily asked, but my father-in-law would only slowly shake his head to my hesitant question. I gratefully bowed to my father-in-law's wishes, which seemed to be the sensible thing to do at the time.

The Bronco would have been better suited to Montana, for I felt somewhat like a cowboy high in the saddle who may be riding more than he can handle. So we hired a young man—one who awoke one morning deciding that he didn't want to do what his father did—to drive the Bronco cross-country. He told us he wanted to stop a few places along the way, including Vegas, and we said, "Have a good time." He must have. The Bronco was never right after that.

There is nothing more certain in my life than my wife's love. Her love only went so far, however. She refused to drive the Bronco. "Daddy always bought the biggest whatever. My first bike was so big, I couldn't ride it, couldn't even push it, it was a boy's bike! The luggage he bought for me to go to college was men's luggage!

I couldn't lift it." She was on a roll, and it wasn't altogether humorous. There was still a fairly strong residue of frustration. "He bought my senior prom dress without my seeing it." "Did you like it?" "I hated it." "Did you wear it?" "Yes." He never knew she didn't like the dress. She could never hurt her father. The prom dress and a few dozen other gowns were carefully stored in a plastic bag and hung in the attic. We gave those dresses away.

My in-law's house before...

I thought of my mother who couldn't afford shoes when she was young. She had seven or eight pairs when she died. Each pair was carefully wrapped in tissue paper and stored in its original shoebox. Each sweater was kept in a plastic bag. Most mountain people work hard at life. They tackle it head-on, ask for no concessions, and are appreciative of what they have.

In California, driving by a Volkswagen dealership on Santa Monica Boulevard in our Bronco one morning, my wife called out, "Stop!" There was a white VW van on display. "We're getting it," she said with a finality that meant there was no discussion. "It's foreign," I said with a pang of West Virginia guilt. "You sound like your Dad." She had not said it rudely but just as a statement of fact. As we waited for the papers to sign for the VW van, I continued to express concern about not buying American. "Besides," I said, "It was a gift from your father." My wife, tired of hearing me said, "Get over it." An hour later we were driving a foreign-made vehicle. The VW van would be the first in a string of foreign cars that we would own. The guilt lessened with each one but I still vocalized for weeks a residue of guilt. The loss of "Betsy"— our nickname for the Olds—to the NYC auction block, then the final death of the resurrected Pontiac, and now trading in the

A BETTER PLACE

...*and after my father-in-law's improvements.*

Bronco, put me another step away from West Virginia and closer to that foreign sports car I had secretly but guiltily coveted.

The picture of a large red brick house that my father-in-law as a young boy had cut out and pasted into a scrapbook was not unlike the very real red brick house that he would later build. He wanted, my father-in-law wrote; "a fairly good size brick bungalow with awnings over a porch." Having money allowed him to expand on the bungalow. He took pride in his house, one that took up more space than any of the neighbors' houses. He delighted in relating to my carpenter father that the redwood paneling in the kitchen was real redwood from the West Coast. The kitchen walls and ceiling were redwood, as was the family room.

Ross had gone about enlarging their house much to the consternation of Claudeis, who was quite happy with the white frame house they had. But the doctor insisted on vastly enlarging the house and covering it in brick, never asking what his wife wanted. My mother-in-law would complain that, "no wonder I can't find anyone, this house is like a maze." She felt encapsulated and kept the barbs coming: "The carpet men thought it was an apartment building." "The refrigerator man thought it was a school; all we need is a flagpole." For the doctor, the house was for his family—at least that is what he maintained. But my wife says he built it for bragging rights. I think in some way he was compensating for being gone so much of the time, for being raised in abject poverty, for taking his dream far beyond what he initially envisioned, for being insecure, and for being a slave to the thing he loved most, being a doctor.

Though the doctor wanted his children to be enlightened, to go out and conquer the world, he at the same time marveled that his children would ever want to leave such a house. The doctor wanted you to enjoy his house, to make yourself comfortable. He loved the house that he built, was very proud of it. It was the only real home he had. But the doctor's passion was doctoring at the hospital he built in Wyoming County, West Virginia. He had been anxious to go into practice for himself. "If I can do it for others, I can do it for myself." My father-in-law's hospital was the only one in that remote part of southern West Virginia. He would treat anyone who walked through the door. At home, patients called night and day. At times they waited outside his house for free medicine and advice that he would give them unsparingly. These people didn't have much, and they didn't expect much. Many were coal miners, and he could always count on seeing a few of them in the hospital, especially after a rowdy weekend.

The commute from his home in Beckley was long, made longer by the mountain road. Many nights he would sleep over. This was because he wanted his family to stay in Beckley, a larger town with better schools. But his heart was in the hospital. It was in the instruments—like my father's carpenter's tools—that he wielded with such precision. It was in the hospital stories that he would eagerly tell, usually during a rare meal with his family. He delighted in relating details of a particularly gruesome operation. It was a typically late night for Ross at the hospital when he tripped and fell down a flight of stairs. He needed numerous transfusions at a time when the nation's blood safety was at risk. He developed cancer shortly thereafter, never telling us this and choosing not to prolong his misery.

The night before he died at age 84, Ross attended a medical meeting to give a talk on some medical procedures. He had a cerebral hemorrhage that night in his bedroom with an open medical journal lying across his chest. He succumbed in a hospital the next day. For the longest time, I didn't see the side of my father-in-law that my wife and her mother would complain about. I just assumed it must be hard to be a good doctor, plus a good husband and a good father. Doctoring, like acting, can be a selfish profession. My mother-in-law wrote; "The only vacations we took were to medical meetings, and your father would always stop for a haircut or Rotary meeting, usually in some dried up place with no shade."

Ironically, as much as he enjoyed his home, he didn't require anything more than a cot and chair and his medical books with a good apple to munch on. Medicine was sort of a meditation for him, a home for his heart and soul. The hospital was where my father-in-law was most grounded, most centered, at peace, at home. My mother-in-law found her home in language. Books made her life worth living. She would comment on the lack of the reading prowess of some politicians. Her love of reading has been passed to my wife and to a lesser but just as appreciated extent, to me. When not reading she filled her time the way many other West Virginian women do. She was an excellent seamstress and made many of my wife's clothes. She ran her church's Sunday school program and also several volunteer groups. Her garden was an inspiration for me. The many weekly letters and phone calls that she and my wife exchanged were full of easy conversation, a delightful give and take, and were an important component of home. Many times when together, they would laugh so hard at something that it brought tears to their eyes. My wife has nurtured a like exchange with our children.

My wife and I cannot imagine my father living anywhere but West Virginia. Her father did not seem nearly so attached to the land, but something kept him there, and it wasn't just his patients. He worked hard to create a persona, and was one of the kindest, most complicated persons I've ever known. In life, I never knew a man who on the surface at least was seemingly so content with where and what he was; and he never hinted that he was interested in looking back. He was quietly judgmental and come hell or high water would not budge from his beliefs. Why did my father-in-law come back to Appalachia? Was it the job that his sister had told him about? Was it because he wanted to be near his beloved sister and brothers? It was all of these, and as for many Appalachians, he couldn't imagine living anywhere else.

When my wife and I came back to her parent's house from her mother's funeral, we both knew then that the house was like most other empty houses, only a little larger. As we sorted through her parents' lives, I was taken aback by how lonely we felt, like strangers as we gathered items to take with us. It was the books I always found myself going through on my visits to my in-laws, and now, what to do with them all? Some we took; the rest we gave away. There was only so much physical baggage from her past that my wife wanted. Some items from her parent's house we shipped, the rest went to an auction we didn't attend. All this is nothing new. This is what sons and daughters do.

Ideally a home offers protection and healing. It gives us the chance to express ourselves. It gives us a place to be restored. But when there is no life, there is no home—just a house. We sold my wife's parents' house after a year, but it was quickly back on the market, like an orphan, waiting hopefully for a family that would stay and love it. One to whom it could provide a haven.

Somewhere I read that a hill child understands what draws a person to live at the ocean. Some are drawn to the mountains as some are drawn to the sea. I was mulling this over as I was driving my three children south into West Virginia after flying to Pittsburgh, Pennsylvania. It was 1984 and we were traveling to attend my father-in-law's funeral. We had rented a car because I thought the drive south to Beckley would be a good chance for my children to get a refresher course on West Virginia. I could regale them with stories about how long it used to take to make the drive before there were interstate highways. "The horse and buggy days, Dad?" On that day when the Avis representative in the Pittsburgh Airport asked what size car I wanted, I looked at my children and thought what my father-in-law would say. I said, "I want the biggest, strongest car you've got." The efficient, business-like Avis person said, "How about a Bronco?"

13

THE OTHER SIDE OF THE MOUNTAIN

When West Virginians leave their island they may not have a job, they may have some doubt about the world, but they go with a freshness of spirit, a sense of wonder about the world. In New York many years ago, a man looked at me for a beat as though I had some coal dust on my face, "You look like you just got off the bus." Actually I had just gotten off the train, and it would be a few years before my first plane ride. His words brought my mother's deer-like eyes in headlights before me. Like Mom, I spent an inordinate amount of time being insecure, apart from some inner place and peace. It took a few years of pain and doubt for me to make a home where the love of my family was unequivocal, where I could rejoice in that love and know that it would carry me over the mountain. Somewhere along the line, because of my wife and children, I made a decision to embrace home and take life as it came. That helped me confront my mother's death and 9-11, and helped me retrace my steps back to West Virginia.

As a young man, the farthest south I had ever been was to visit my wife at her college in Lynchburg, Virginia. It was the first time I had been out of West Virginia by myself. There had been two other crossings of the border, but those had been with friends. In those days there were no bright wide interstates in West Virginia so it was a major trip to get to its borders—unless I was venturing (and we rarely did) over into Pennsylvania, which was only ten or so miles down the road from Morgantown. As a young mountaineer, I found it a wonder of living in West Virginia yet being so close to Pennsylvania. Ohio was the west for me. California was another world. I was ignorant of everything that wasn't West Virginian and fairly ignorant of a lot of things that were West Virginian. I didn't arrive at Randolph Macon Women's College until after dark and after "lock down"—the girls couldn't go out after 11 P.M. But I was treated like any other young man who came to visit his sweetheart. I was told to take a seat in the "parlor." My wife-to-be came down, and we had a few minutes together before she had to return to her room. It was sort of like visiting a white-collar prisoner.

My perception of Virginia as the more affluent, sophisticated, snooty neighbor resulted in my somewhat self-conscious feeling upon entering the mother state. It wasn't that I was a bare-footed hillbilly or thought of myself in that light or had ever heard anyone referred to in that manner, but I was not bursting with self-assurance crossing that border. I recall an interview when I was a relatively young actor. I had taken my first cross-country flight for a meeting in Los Angeles at Twentieth Century Fox. I was in a large office with the producer, director and star of an upcoming film that I was being considered for. During the session I noticed I had a big hole in my sweater. The sweater was one I had had since high school. Thinking of my mother, I spent the whole interview trying to cover up the hole. When people asked me how the interview went, I could only recall the hole in my sweater.

Everything seemed perfect in the well-kept, quiet, gentle little town of Lynchburg. Lynchburg is a town where even Garrison Keillor's *Prairie Home Companion* is on too late, making it a suitable home for Jerry Falwell's Liberty College. There was a feeling of the old Commonwealth, the aristocracy. Southerners were from a different world and were suspect. My self-consciousness seemed to melt beside the assurance of the beautiful, tall, blond, blue-eyed girl I had come to see. Such beauty can be rather intimidating but she made me feel so at ease. She was, I thought, way above my station in life. I didn't know anyone like her. She was smarter, better educated, worldly, and so sophisticated. Her accent was soft. Mine had a twang. She had even been to Europe one summer on her own. This was utterly beyond my comprehension. I didn't know anyone, had never heard of anyone, who had been to Europe. I did have a recollection of seeing a slide show a man in my town gave of his travels to Europe. This unfortunately did not dispel my awkwardness and ignorance in conversations with my intended. I was as bland as a pile of dirt.

The properness of the all-woman campus made me slightly uncomfortable. Was this what they called a finishing school? No, my intended's friends laughed, "That's Sweet Briar. If you want rich, go to Sweet Briar; if you want a party girl go to Hollins." "What do you get at Randolph Macon?" The girls laughed again and said, "A wife." You also got smart. How could this intelligent beauty possibly want to be seen with me? I was from West Virginia. But wait a minute—so was she! I was somewhat of a loner, not a lot of laughs, and unbelievably innocent—not the sort of tailor-made beau for the girl I was courting. To top it off, I had no money and had this secret desire to be an actor. Then again, I didn't smoke or chew or drink. I didn't hunt, didn't own a gun, didn't fish, and didn't play pinball. So perhaps there was hope.

My wife would later tell me that she had never been happy at Randolph-Macon Women's College. It was her father's school of choice for her. Unknown to her at the time, he filled out her Randolph-Macon application. There was no discussion or consideration of any other school. She felt unprepared and isolated there. She thought the other southern ladies were more sophisticated and better educated than her. I couldn't imagine. My wife spent her college years in the stacks of the library, ever studying trying to measure up for her father. She measured up very well but questions whether the toll was worth it. She always seemed to know who she was. I saw no reason why she would have a doubt about anything except perhaps for the hayseed she was about to marry. I am glad but mystified why she never had a doubt about me.

Going to my future wife's home in Beckley was also different, and somewhat awkward for me. The most unsettling thing for me visiting her home for the first time was finding a framed charcoal etching in the entry hall of Robert E. Lee, the famous southern general. As soon as you entered the house, Lee greeted you. Lee had been the enemy! He fought for Virginia! Lee had turned down Lincoln's offer to lead the Union troops. He and his troops had been turned back at Cheat Mountain, not too far from where Dad built his childhood cabin. I knew Beckley was in the southern part of the state, but this rather grand house belonged in Virginia! I was in turmoil. I knew that I had to be on my guard, especially if they found out I was a Yankee sympathizer. I felt like a turncoat.

My lovely wife, Chip, as a cheerleader for Woodrow Wilson High School in Beckley, WV.

My wife-to-be told me her mother was from Louisiana. She was a history buff, but there was not much discussion of Lincoln. Let me clarify that; there was no discussion of Lincoln. In Louisiana there had been men willing to fight for the Union, but I didn't know this then and certainly wouldn't have dared mentioned it anyway.

My in-laws'-to-be home was the largest house I had ever been in. It was beautiful, with a sunroom and dining room and a large shaded back yard. There was even a sitting room that was full of books and a family room full of more books and a library with nothing but books. There were books on tabletops and bedside tables. I had never seen books in a house before. I never knew anyone before who bought books. It was the first home that I had ever been in that had a library and a reading room. It seemed as though my mother-in-law always had a book in her hand. She was always discussing the latest book she had read or was reading, usually having to do with history or biography. When my future mother-in-law waxed on about all the English kings, I would listen, but in those days I never would take part in a discussion with her about books out of fear of exposing the dunderhead that I thought I was. It was the books that made the strongest statement about my soon-to-be in-laws, that and their kindness to me.

Somehow, I guess I didn't come across as a hopeless northern carpetbagger. I was made to feel welcome in their home and accepted. I was in love with their daughter and wanted them to accept me, but also I needed their acceptance for myself. My father-in-law was a little skeptical about his daughter marrying someone he had only met a few times and who wanted to be an actor, but he never once was anything but kind to me. As we left their home on our wedding day, he was standing in the entry crying hard over the realization that his daughter was gone. I think back to one of his letters we later found that he had written to his future wife. "Tell your mother that under no circumstances will you be returning. Be definite." I was very proud and touched when he became a fan and had my picture on his office desk. My wife says he showed it to everybody.

After we married and ventured out of state, I tended to be just a little wide-eyed. As we passed into each new state, I would have my bride take my picture. I bought little souvenirs at each stop. My lack of sophistication, ignorance, and curiosity seemed boundless. In St. Peter's Church in New Orleans, I saw a man exit a door at the back of the church, "There's the bathroom," I confided to my wife. She commenced laughing so hard she had to leave the church. I followed her, and when she could finally control herself, she told me that was the door to the confessional. She really had a hayseed on her hands. If people were concerned about the painting *West Virginia Moon* being an embarrassment to the state, then God knows what they would have thought of me. I was a walking hillbilly billboard.

Many West Virginians must leave the state in order to find a life. Others feel they have earned a stake in their place. They have toiled and fought and suffered with the vigor and dignity of their ancestors, and this makes it hard to let go, to leave—so they stay and work to make West Virginia better. I never consciously considered leaving until I was in college. Maybe I had to leave West Virginia to get some sort of perspective. I don't mean that I lamented any backwardness of the place. I was too consumed with myself at the time to be aware of much else. Self indulgence, God, what a curse. This country is tortured by it. I had not, as yet, read Harry Caudill's *Night Comes To The Cumberlands*. I didn't feel any coldness or jealousy or any other negatives. The landscape complimented the people. I didn't feel the people unworthy of the land.

After I graduated from college in business, I had secured a handful of job interviews. One was with Kroger, a grocery chain. However, a personnel test convinced them that it would not be a match made in heaven. After a couple of other similar interviews, my insecurity was healthy as a weed and growing as fast. I knew all these companies were right and had actually done me a favor. If Kroger had offered me a job, I might never have left West Virginia. I would have stayed because, though I was a heavy daydreamer and was restless, there was that part in me that is in most West Virginians, a feeling of not being able to imagine a life beyond the mountains. Looking back I must have surely doubted my West Virginia "rugged individualism and courage," but somewhere in me was the feeling that change, frightening as it was,

was a necessity and something that I had been dreaming about for so long. I had to leave home but I would for the longest time, be coming and going.

Kroger was smart not to hire me, but I was left with a dearth of choices until I came across a bulletin at West Virginia University with a listing of assistantships available at a Midwest school that was unidentified. Complicating my unspoken desire to be an actor was the misplaced ambition of wanting to achieve a higher academic degree. I had managed a Master's degree. The notion of learning, though, wasn't nearly as important as the degree. I was doing everything I could to pass as being educated. I needed certificates of authenticity. I had been running from something, fear of not amounting to anything—afraid that a forecast made by an older neighborhood friend that I would flunk out of college in a year would come true.

In a quandary as to what to do, I sent away a graduate school application and a short while later received a call from one Earl Bradley in the Speech Department at Southern Illinois University. Unbeknownst to me, a friend from West Virginia University was a graduate student there and had seen my application on Dr. Bradley's desk and recommended me. Dr. Bradley offered me an assistantship over the phone and told me that my wife could probably receive an assistantship in the English department, which she did. So on my wife's strength and her confidence and love, we struck out together. I knew, when I hitched the U-haul on the back of my wife's red hardtop Oldsmobile and we headed west for graduate assistantships at a school we knew nothing about, that I was on my way to my life's adventure. What made it possible was that I was not alone.

We arrived at our destination of Southern Illinois University in Carbondale, Illinois, called Little Egypt. Shortly after settling into classes at the doctorate level I began to feel what Auden's poem "The Age of Anxiety," perhaps expresses. It is, as Paul Tillich writes, "the anxiety of not being able to preserve one's own being which underlies every fear and is the frightening element in it."[1] This is an anxiety with which West Virginians are all somewhat familiar with as they struggle to maintain what they hold near and dear. It is the kind of anxiety you can contain for only so long. I ended up in my parents' living room in a chair, peeling tinfoil off Juicy Fruit chewing gum wrappers. This was while my wife and I were back in West Virginia on Christmas vacation from graduate school. It had been my first lengthy time away from West Virginia, and perhaps a pretend life was catching up to me. My youthful fears and the angst from trying to prove myself could no longer be contained, it seemed, and were being exhibited I felt in a most unflattering and shameful way.

Continuing going to school was not a planned trip. We had no two-year or ten-year plan. We sort of climbed the ladder and jumped into the lake of fate. It was as though when buying a bus ticket and the man says "Where to?" You have no idea. "Where does the bus end up?" That is where we went. Sometimes choices are shrouded in mystery. Are they random or destined? I don't know if my ancestors had a destination in mind. They did, like us, like the Latinos, want a better life. So you just go, scrambled emotions and all. You find a place you think can work, and you settle. Happenstances are a part of life. A burr attaches itself to your pant leg and hitches a ride until it drops off somewhere to sprout anew, over and over and over.

To arrive somewhere you have to leave the place you've been. Without my wife, I don't know that I would have had the courage to strike out on my own. A man needs a strong woman. Back in those days, a woman's place was behind her man, to follow him and support him. I was selfish though I didn't realize it. My wife, I unconsciously assumed, would walk beside me supporting my needs, my career. Perhaps she assumed this also, and she grew very adept at swinging from vine to vine while juggling children, husband and building her own life. It's hard to deal with real life alone. It would not have been possible for me. I needed to create a place with somebody. Being afraid, I needed somebody to hold my hand, to not settle down as it were but to be with me. I have been blessed with the strength, grace, and love of my wife. My wife and I would be a team of sorts, a pair forming the beginnings of our home. It took me a while to appreciate the joys and benefits of a partnership, of creating a home together. We would learn to push our individual boundaries and find a common ground to live.

A BETTER PLACE

My adorable wife Chip.

Later, living in New York City, a real estate listing caught my eye: "19th century Victorian farmhouse with barn on three acres." The house was located on the side of a hill in the midst of many sweet-smelling tall pines flush with cones. I loved the land at first sight and bought it, not even going inside the house and never considering whether my wife would like it or not. I just assumed she would. I raced back to New York City, found my wife and young son on the playground in Central Park. We hurried back up the Saw Mill River Parkway to the small town of Pleasantville, New York. When my wife saw the house and the land, she commented that it reminded her of West Virginia. That impulsive purchase was our first house. Prior to this, there had been an assortment of apartments that were basically holding pens while we awaited our next move.

The day we took possession, the owner was standing forlornly alone in the yard saying goodbye to a place he loved. His wife told us the story of two sisters who had been the first owners. They sold eggs, chickens, and rabbits at the bottom of the long steep driveway where my father-in-law would later talk me into erecting two stone pillars: "They'll set the property off, make a grand entrance." When the stone pillars were finished, he exclaimed, "My, don't they look grand." They are still standing, and this brings a laugh to both my wife and me as we wonder if the current owners have slid their cars into those stone pillars as often as we did during a winter's snow.

As the sisters' story went, there was a man who would pass by in his carriage on a regular basis and buy eggs and chickens from them. He became quite fond of one of the sisters and she of him, so much so that she rode off with him one day to the end of Bear Ridge Road where he lived in a big house with his wife. The sister lived there as part of a threesome for the rest of her life, and the sister who was left behind and alone became a recluse and stopped working the farm, never selling another thing at the bottom of the drive. There had been, as Joyce Carol Oates said, "…a sad story." But the land was still fertile, the barn standing, and the county didn't own it because of back taxes. There was the spirit of a lonely heart on a hill amidst the tall pine trees. I retrieved an old sign in the barn and posted it on the driveway. It read "Locust Grove Farm."

Making a place frames a great deal of a life. It was at our first house that I planted my first garden, learned how to build a stone wall. *The New York Times Book of Home Repair* was my Bible, but it was growing up in West Virginia as a carpenter's son that taught me and shaped me and prepared me for my role as a general handyman. As a teenager though, I wanted to stay in bed on summer mornings rather than heed Dad's call to go with him as his "hand me this, hand me that" helper. The time moved slowly on those days. And now there I was proudly pointing out to him the work I had done on my own house.

Besides an addition (that Dad helped me build while Mom swept up piles of sawdust) every room was painted and or wallpapered, molding was installed, new floors were laid, new light fixtures were installed, bathrooms were tiled, and bookshelves were built. When we had been graduate assistants, my wife and I could receive books from publishers for free. I sent for all I could. Sometimes two or three books would arrive on the same day, books, like the ones in my in-laws' house. I treasured every one and to this day still have a few. The first set of books that we bought while still graduate students was the *Encyclopedia Britannica*. I still enjoy referring to it.

Eventually I would build a pretty basic tree house on the hill behind our house for our children—though they hardly ever used it. My wife rightly pointed out that I built it for myself. I have always tried to create personal spaces. As a child I would erect a blanket between two chairs and make a world. As a young boy of ten or eleven, I would sit and bounce my head against the back of the davenport and singsong out loud. Eventually I wore a bald spot the size of a quarter on the back of my head. Efforts were made to keep me from bouncing, but a bald spot on the back of my head was a small price to pay for that sanctuary.

Years later my son would have the same ritual only on a spring hobbyhorse. His was also a nightly routine. My wife and I can still hear his loud and joyful songs exuberantly replaying the day's events. There was something tribal and ancient about his putting his days into song. He rode so hard that we were fearful he would catapult out the window. Finally the horse broke. My wife and I panicked, but we found a man who welded new parts and soon our son was riding once again, joyfully oblivious to everything else, singing his way into the sunset of his day.

It was in the tree house that I became a bird watcher. I recall my excitement on seeing my first pileated woodpecker. My mother-in-law was a devoted bird watcher. She gave me my first bird book, one of several she gave me. Bird watching, like fishing, requires patience, and I learned much from my mother-in-law, who was forced to learn patience as a result of being married to a doctor. She taught me everything from the kind of feed and flowers different birds liked, to the feeders to use, along with hints about keeping squirrels away. She kept a slingshot at her window and had marbles for ammunition in order to keep the pigeons and squirrels at bay. She actually hit a pigeon once, knocking it out.

My wife and I put up birdhouses and all kinds of feeders and even lint from the dryer and straw to aid the birds in building their homes. I knew every square foot of the three acres, and all the birds and animals that lived there with us. I picked raspberries and blackberries every season. We planted pumpkins that overtook our garden. I delighted in cutting firewood, sledding down the hills with my children, raking huge piles of leaves and remodeling and expanding, with Dad's guiding hands, the house and barn. Most if not all of these ingredients of home were made possible because of my West Virginia upbringing.

All had been right with our world, when suddenly, on a beautiful summer day, I was hit with a doomed feeling of panic and found myself in a hospital's emergency room for what would be the first of many visits. "It's not a heart attack?" Eventually I was diagnosed with a panic disorder. A doctor gave me books to read on anxiety and prescribed Xanax. I don't like taking pills. The doctor said, "If you're cold, you put on a jacket, don't you?" I was ready to put on a hooded fur-lined parka and gloves even though by then we were living in southern California. I did eventually acknowledge problems that I had long been aware of ever since leaving West Virginia.

In some small way, perhaps my adventure upon leaving West Virginia seemed as daunting and reckless to me as the one my ancestors took two centuries before. I cannot begin to imagine what that life was like for my ancestors. Leaving England,

A BETTER PLACE

My wife Chip, with her first car.

Scotland and Hungary when they did could not have been easy. Leaving is never easy, as exhilarating as it may be filled with dread. Choice involves pain. It was my mother, in effect, who put my coat on and gently pushed me out the door, watching me go with her face pressed against the glass. Leaving my parents' house was a way of testing myself. What was I made of? Was I a man?

The hard part hadn't been leaving my parent's home; it was leaving West Virginia. My oneness with West Virginia made it hard in retrospect for me to assimilate outside of West Virginia. Roy Harmon, one-time poet laureate of West Virginia, wrote: "So bless the hills, and toss your traveling shoes\ Away –and cultivate some peace of mind\ All happiness that any man can use\ Is here—so don't be selfish—and don't be blind." I was probably both selfish and blind and stupid, and it was all coming home to roost in an emotional upheaval for which I finally admitted I needed help. I had let wanderlust cloud my days. But West Virginia wouldn't let me run away from it; and the more I learned about it, I knew it was a place I'd never lose.

Breece D'J Pancake, who wrote so wonderfully and true about life in the West Virginia mountains, according to James McPherson, found it difficult at the University of Virginia: "His middle-class West Virginia origins tended to isolate him from the much more sophisticated and worldly middle-class students from the suburbs of Washington and the Northeast, as well as from the upper-class students of southern background."[2] I did not circulate in rarified circles, though like Pancake I may have on some level desired their approval. Today I am still not really at ease in any kind of country club setting. I avoid such places. There was a need to be perfect because there was no time to be imperfect. "Make us look good." I took whatever affirmation and or distraction I could find so as to not think, to find some way of calming myself, to convince myself that I really mattered even if I wasn't perfect.

Like Pancake, I tended to be somewhat self-conscious about the poverty in West Virginia. A residue of inferiority hung over me, like an ill-fitting suit. This insecurity, while certainly causing me problems, did not deter me because my wife would not allow it. My family is not, I think, as convinced of my professed joyful attitude toward life as I am. They have reason. They have witnessed me do battle with life. Like mother like son, I have been unable to rest, to simply have fun for fun's sake, to sit on the porch and have a conversation about nothing, just talk and talk, or not. I have had to learn how to do nothing.

In our family, I am known for rearranging furniture, a set designer at heart. I can be perfectly happy lugging furniture from room to room, re-hanging pictures, painting a wall, scrubbing a floor, all while my wife is out of the house. It must have made mother happy whenever she would finish washing down the house. I recently came across a few old eight-millimeter home movies that I had not realized existed. One of my daughters on viewing them said that she had never seen me having such fun as I was having in those home movies. I was throwing snowballs. The robust laughter on my face was shocking, and I was very relieved because I knew or thought I knew that my childhood, if distracted, had been a reasonably happy one. So why had I become a nervous worry wart, fighting myself to get through the day, hanging on to the toilet seat, a bit of a fatalist? Perhaps children in West Virginia don't understand that they are like most people who walk that tightrope. They need to know that there is a light, and it will get brighter. There is a future out there waiting for them to put their arms around.

We all deal with fears and specifically with the fear of death. The writer Alice Thomas Ellis in her lovely book *A Welsh Childhood*, wrote that she seemed to have

> *thought, all my life of little but death—partly perhaps because of impatience, a yearning to have it over and done with: that extraordinary last thing that we are called upon to do, the act of dying...mostly it comes from the old awareness that I am not whole, that there is something missing: something more important than all the world. Death is the price we must pay for completion.*[3]

There have been accounts of people taking their lives after losing loved ones on September 11th. Perhaps in some way they felt their life was over, completed. On nearing the age of twenty, I was consumed with the dark, the ultimate dark of death. Death was something for other people to think about, older people. I was too young to think about being old. So why was I so aware of time, of death? I never wore a watch for years because I couldn't comprehend how fast time was moving and yet how slow my life was.

You play the hand you're dealt. Somewhere along the line, it all became too much for Pancake, and he took his own life. Perhaps his truth would not allow otherwise. It is no coincidence that West Virginia suicide numbers rank among the highest in the nation. Life's moments are as fleeting as they are beautiful. Alice Thomas Ellis continued, "We all have to do time, and it is both unwise and ungrateful to yearn only for eternity." Is that what my fear was about, a yearning for eternity? Forget eternity, just experience life, as it is now—which is what my wife has tried to teach me. I kept silent and proud, putting on a façade to hide my helplessness and fear. There was no choice but to acknowledge both, for time cruises on unconcerned with eternity. The children of West Virginia need to know that none of us are secure. Some of us are just better actors.

For the longest time after I left West Virginia, every place was a stopover on the way to somewhere else. It seemed I was never satisfied wherever I was. I searched the real estate pages of newspapers and magazines to find the idealistic home, the idyllic picture that said this was a home I could live in, a home maybe with a white picket fence, a fenced-in pasture in Lexington, Kentucky, the white birches of Vermont, the white clouds over San Francisco. Perhaps I was looking for the white clapboard house on Ridgeway Avenue in Morgantown. Home was for so long everywhere but where I was; Big Sur, Minneapolis, New Mexico, Montreal, Houston, Bucks County, Charleston, S.C., apartments in London, Paris, wherever we have been. There always seemed to be something about those places that made me think "wouldn't it be nice to live here."

Before we moved to California, I was constantly looking with an admiring eye to the picturesque villages of New England. I subscribed to *Yankee Magazine*, and each month they would feature a house for sale. There were very few that didn't appeal to me. Even after relocating to Los Angeles, I persuaded my wife into going back to New England to look at a couple of houses. I was like a lover flitting from one relationship to another, never knowing what he wants, never knowing what he has. And yet as I yearned for some place, I was afraid that if I should stumble upon that Garden of Eden, I wouldn't recognize it. So what was I looking for or running from?

Could the answer perhaps be in both cases West Virginia? I once flirted with buying a farm in West Virginia, but our children have all become, as I told Dad, confirmed Californians. This was hard to tell Dad and at first hard to admit to myself. Only a short time ago, Dad expressed his concern for my oldest daughter, who lives near the center where an earthquake had just occurred: "You oughta move back to West Virginia." Unlike Dad, I don't think I really fell in love with the story of West Virginia, its land and its people, until I was gone. After leaving, I realized how much the land and its people, and their love, have meant to me.

One day, having just refinished the second-floor bedroom doors of our New York house and having split several cords of wood for the coming winter, my youngest daughter had said referring to a coming event, "Is he coming?"—"he" being me. I was heartbroken and sadly looked to my wife who gently but firmly said, "We're moving to California." I had never thought of actually moving to California. "But this is home," I said. "Home is where we are," my wife replied. Our suburban New York farmhouse, with all the care and love we gave it, my attachment to it, how could we walk away? It did seem I was becoming a commuter to California. I was gone from home a lot for work and thus was spending less time with my family. Often I would be gone for long stretches of time, usually in the winter when my wife would be left to cope with the snow and the children and the house. I was letting my work be my home, succumbing to the idea that it was enough if I provided for them and they had a nice house to live in.

My wife lived that scenario with her father and knew the toll that it took on her family. For me the house was a place of joy, a retreat, a place that I was so attached to yet was spending more and more time away from. In those years I would walk off the plane in Los Angeles and it was magic. My responsibilities were 3,000 miles away. After returning from a West Coast trip, I would find that each family member would have to readjust to my being home again. Two weeks after my wife's pronouncement that we were moving, I hung the refinished doors back on their hinges and was off to California for work and to find shelter for my family. I was never in that New York house again. It was a place that had been good to us. Friends had a picture painted of the house and sent it to us.

My wife loved that first house in New York, though I think I found it harder to sell than she. Letting go, as they say, is such sweet sorrow. My wife has always been good at living in the here and now, in the moment. She has a "the future will take care of itself" frame of mind. It is from my wife that I have learned that it is the present that is important; it is there that our relationship found a depth of solitude that has served us and our marriage through a couple of briar patches. Home has kept me busy and grounded and loved in order to withstand self-destruction. And September 11, 2001, was a reminder that it is hard to do anything but live in the here and now.

I never dreamed about living in Los Angeles, but finally that is where we found another house on another hill, a hill that was reminiscent of some far away hills of West Virginia. Though I feel I am beyond that child with his nose pressed to the car window, who sees the expanse and wants it, I still find myself browsing real estate windows looking at the country houses for sale—only the search is a real, contained search within central California. It has been in Los Angeles oddly enough that I have come to realize what my wife always knew, that home is not a house. I had forgotten, if I ever knew, that being together is the most important thing. At first, in Los Angeles, we rented from a man who owned Rent-A-Wreck, a car rental place. He also owned rent-a-wreck houses, it seemed. We ended up in one because it was the only place that was somewhat furnished and would take three children, two dogs and a cat and was affordable. There had to have been a few sad stories attached to this place, but we made it easily through a year in a long-abused house that I was told had a good address. Too many tenants had passed its walls, most leaving no clues of their passing, and location could not warm the coldness of this motel-house. However, you put in an abundance of family love and vitality and hope, and the coldest place comes to life.

My family flourished in California. Soon after we moved to L.A., my wife found a whole new challenging and invigorating life as she became very involved with the non-profit sector, providing services for those who needed them. She has headed, in a non-paid full time position as president, a multi-million dollar non-profit that services thousands of people every year. She, as president of another non-profit, has helped many homeless and abused women and their children. In a large community like L.A., her efforts were appreciated, and she has been honored, I proudly say, a number of times. I only write this, knowing it will embarrass her, because it is an example of how one person can still make a difference in this high speed, high definition modern world. My wife is an example, following in the long tradition of women caregivers. This assumption that it is the woman that can afford not to be paid is something that our society has depended on and taken advantage of over the years, and is a statement about how women are still viewed.

I have grown appreciative of Los Angeles and southern

California and am thankful for the day my wife looked at me with love and announced that we were moving. We eventually bought a house in the Toluca Lake section of Los Angeles, a charming area. There is a lake that we eventually got a glance of as it is hidden behind some expensive houses. We did get to see Bob Hope occasionally drive down our street on his way to the Lakeside Country Club. He never failed to wave. I was always thrilled to see him and return his wave. My father loved Bob Hope, and I was ever hopeful that Dad would visit and get to wave to Mr. Hope. I held the possibility out as a carrot to my father. He didn't bite.

The Toluca Lake house's best feature was a large front yard—which I kept mowed despite my neighbor's taunts—and where a rare fruit-bearing chestnut tree resided. People would knock on our door asking if they could make reservations for chestnut-picking season. They loved the chestnuts, and we loved the tree. As is the fashion in L.A., we decided to sell this house shortly after we bought it. In my West Virginia boyhood, when a house was put up for sale that meant the people had left town or had died. I never knew anyone who ever moved from my old neighborhood. In Los Angeles it seemed like everyone moved or was considering a move. They were "moving up." This tendency to regard houses as seemingly little more than a place to park was disconcerting but slightly amusing. I told my wife we would never find another place like the one we had in New York—the place that reminded us of West Virginia.

My wife called me one day and said she saw a house she liked. "Do you want to see it?" "No," I said, "buy it. You never saw the New York one." So she bought it, and when I finally went to look at it, prepared of course to not like it—how could it possibly compare to New York—I made a non-appreciated remark about the house needing a lot of work. My wife asked me, "What does it remind you of?" I smiled and told her it reminded me of our place in New York, being that it was on a hill with lots of trees and enough land to garden to my heart's content. We kissed a kiss that reverberated back to West Virginia. My wife laughed and said, "Yes, I knew you would like it."

The place spoke to us. It would be more than a place to park. Coincidently, as with the New York house, again we were the third owners. The first owner here had been a greens man for a local golf club. He had planted a wide array of plants and trees on the property. The second owners had done some work on the house, and it was, I had to admit, in fairly good shape. There didn't appear to have been any sad stories. We have since created a place that for us is pretty nearly an ideal environment. The name of our street is Encanto, which I learned meant 'enchanted' in Spanish.

There is a visage of a small town feel in our area of Sherman Oaks, California. I can walk to the paper stand, restaurant and just about anything else. Yet the rather hectic pace of life seems a little unreal. While there are more people, I don't know many of them. There is a sort of anonymity in Sherman Oaks, let alone greater Los Angeles. You can just pass through and never get very involved. You can force yourself to stare straight ahead and never see the Latinos on the curb.

On our land in the Sherman Oaks hills there are many squirrels, a couple of skunks, a few possum, an occasional deer and coyote, snakes, and two rabbits that by outwitting our dogs, have been hanging around for several years. There seems to be an abundance of rats, mice, gophers and lizards. I have attracted a wide assortment of birds with feeders, birdhouses, fountains and many plants and trees to feed on—my own little patch of West Virginia. One marvels at the well-designed compact cup of a nest the hummingbird builds. The hummingbirds and I have become friends. Butterflies and bees abound, along with all sorts of insects. The spider webs are too numerous for my children, our youngest proclaiming, "It's them or me." But she too appreciates the intricacies of their webs and the intricacies of home. All of these denizens never cease to bring joy. To a point, I am on a friendlier basis with the denizens of our land than I am with my neighbors, though when the 1994 earthquake hit, immediate neighbors called on each other to assess personal and property damage. It would be nice, people said at the time, to see more of each other, and not just at earthquake time.

In the Odyssey it is written: "Each day I long for home, long for the sight of home." My wife and I worked and improvised together and tried to build a place, a home, a life together, though it was my independent West Virginia wife—wiser, stronger, and more mature—who maintained a place with, as she inscribed on a picture of herself that she gave me not long after we first met, "faith, hope, and charity." I think it helped that we came from the same area; we shared the same values. Home is a centered place where our family can touch and hold and know each other even when far apart and where we learn from each other. Home gives us a place to be restored. Home is comprised of the same stories we read aloud to each other every Christmas. Home is the Hungarian nut-roll my wife and daughters make from a recipe handed down from my mother's mother. The brown sugar and butter, walnuts and raisins are carefully folded into a roll. The nut-roll expresses something about our lives, our home.

Wherever my wife and I have lived, I have carried baggage from my roots, an actor dependent on his props. My grandmother Selby's handmade quilt, one of several she made for my family, is on my bed. The hand-etched glass that her sister-in-law gave her when she and Grandpap were married sits on a shelf in our dining room. I recall Grandma rummaging through the smoke house looking for an item she wanted me to have. "Ray would know where it is. It's not fair, when one goes the other should go too." Among various items she found were a German helmet that my father had brought back from the war because his father wanted something from "over there." Grandma told me she had had to scrub and scrub to get the blood out. Grandma found what she was looking for finally; it was a knife my father had made as a child with his initials carved into the handle. I have restored it, and it sits on a shelf in our home on display.

Though I never knew my Dad's grandfather, I have carefully and lovingly carried with us the black walnut bed that he made and that my oldest daughter slept in. I look at the bed and a table that he also made and see his caring skillful hands. I see all my children at one time or another rocking in the child's rocker that their great-great-grandfather built. That child's rocker sits in our bedroom waiting for grandchildren. These "props" not only bring me contentment, but they are connected to the very fiber of who and what I am, along with the baggage of the "unruly mind." There are assorted other "old" items I have gathered from mother's mom. These things that were used by my ancestors give me some continuity. They speak to me and remind me of my grandparents and their lives. The pieces that Dad has lovingly restored I will cherish, and perhaps my children will also.

Life is a process of finding ourselves, individually and together if we are lost or think we're lost or just pretending to be lost. I suppose we are on our way home as we search for the answers we all seek to the meaning of life. On two occasions I have driven up our old driveway in Pleasantville, N.Y., to just look at that first house again, and everything twenty odd years later still looks the same. Remnants of the tree house are still there. The pine trees are still standing tall. But the best thing was sitting in the car with my youngest daughter in that moment and realizing what that moment meant. We talked of memories that were so vivid we had gone back all the way.

My daughter is a beautiful child as are her brother and sister, who on their own each made a pilgrimage back to Locust Grove Farm and knocked on the door. A son of the family we sold it to invited them in, and my daughter took pictures. Their trip back told me that while the tree house might not have the meaning for them that it had for me, there was still for them a sense of place there, and this added to their sense of home. That is also true for my wife, though she has never felt the need to visit. It is someone else's home now.

Each of us must feel a personal responsibility to solve our problems, and by that I mean we must be steadfast in our will and belief and love. Love will make all the difference. So we try to take the moment, to take each day for what we always knew it was—a gift. I now think of home as not so much a tangible place. It is in the fiber of what we are; it is in the marrow of our bones, and we find it over the course of a life in the souls of people who love us. Perhaps the children of war, the curbside Latinos, the homeless, and others in similar situations of necessity learn about home sooner. Perhaps they know that home is not just a roof over your head. They, like myself, miss the family left behind. They miss the support that a society of home can bring.

It was my wife who took me by the hand and taught me how to live outside West Virginia, outside my own little gray cloud of melancholy with a need to beat myself up, outside my inarticulateness, my insecurities and fear. She always would tell me that I knew more than I thought I knew. The older one gets, the more you don't know becomes a little overwhelming, so you get sort of panicked in trying to catch up with the world. We all need to be reminded that we do perhaps know more than we think we do, or we know enough. We just have to have the courage to speak up occasionally. It wasn't easy for my bride, for like my mother, a temper bloomed in me early in my marriage to hide what I can only think was some kind of quiet desperation. My wife didn't reject me, and if she could accept me, then surely others could. The question was could I accept myself? My wife was my inspiration to improve myself, to find ways of expressing myself, to believe that even when you can't understand who or what you are, when you are so afraid, that things are still possible. A future is out there for you.

The struggle was worth it. I know it was for me, and I believe it has been for my wife—at least that's what she tells me. Life continues to be an audition. We were two West Virginians whom it turned out had more in common than I could ever have wished for. Her love has allowed me to endure and isn't that what love is about? Love allows us to carry on. I have remained a dreamer from the hills and occasionally catch myself looking down or up at one of those hills. I later even learned to have an appreciation of Robert E. Lee, despite the battle at Gettysburg. That portrait of Lee that hung in my in-laws' entry now resides in our home in California, albeit alongside a portrait of Lincoln—they bookend a framed early map of Virginia before West Virginia seceded. I can remember my mother-in-law laughing and talking about a recent history she had read of the Civil War. My in-laws' generosity and kindness cannot be overstated. Over the years I became very comfortable in their house. Eventually I even ventured into fun discussions with her about Lincoln and Lee. I looked forward to visiting whenever we could, and my son delighted in talking history with his grandmother.

14

LOOKING AHEAD

The crossroads that America and West Virginia face makes it imperative that, while we may all be strangers, we reach out to one another. Everyone has a right to things such as health and safety. West Virginia and its people need to ponder the challenges. In a small community like West Virginia, where the population today stands at 1,850,000 or so, everyone has to be active in helping each other. We have to expect more of each other. It is one way that a poor state can cope. No one can afford to not speak up in West Virginia. On second thought, I don't think speaking up is a problem. It's just that those with the most money speak loudest.

When people have suffered decades of neglect, when they lack educational skills, when their diet is poor, when they lack money or a job, it is hard if not impossible for them to help others. They are struggling to get themselves and their homes in order. The federal government needs to be more involved getting them on their feet. What did the nineties economy do for West Virginians? Many today are like the Latinos on the curb, living from one payday to the next. One of the things that could be done that would indirectly help West Virginia is for Americans to buy American. My father would agree. The problem is that we are now basically a global economy. It is hard today to exclusively buy clothing, electronics, toys, or housewares that are made in the USA.

The rest of the country has long paid little attention to a group of people who are being displaced, sacrificed for greed, or for—as the coal advertisement says—"keeping the lights on." West Virginia is a type of occupied state with the people at the mercy of the occupiers who will spend millions to promote their agenda. We need to get West Virginia's story out there: the price in human terms that is being paid. If West Virginia is to survive, we have to stand and shout—enough is enough! Boldness is required to make a new start. There has been no national outcry over the injustice that West Virginians have endured. While providing cheap energy for the nation and the world, we are now left with few job choices, high pollution and poverty. West Virginians don't like to complain. They are a proud people.

The governor of West Virginia must make West Virginia's problem a national one. The country needs to be told and made to face the reality of the personal price some are paying for the comfort and convenience of those benefiting from the coal industry. The governor must set a plate at the table of American's conscience.

Boldness may not be good politics. The governor must ask, as Lincoln asked, "What will the people say?" Then he must be willing as Lincoln said, not to "surrender the game leaving any card un-played," and to "hold on with a bull-dog grip and chew and choke as much as possible." Of course one notion is that you can't be elected unless you are aligned with the coal companies. Voters may get impatient, for the process will be long term. Continuing to rely on coal seems to be a death wish, a cheap, if you will, death wish. Most people acknowledge this, and there are efforts afoot to diversify the state's economy.

The severance tax on coal and timber should be increased with the proceeds targeted for the neediest areas. Presently the tax is doled out to the areas with the most population, so the small communities get little benefit from the severance tax. One community received all of $300. Maybe there should be a strike to get a fair share of coal profits, or a revolution to shut down all the mountaintop operations. The government will be forced to invade West Virginia, an armed takeover. And as is well noted, West Virginians will not lay down their guns. There will be casualties. But no one knows where West Virginia is anyway, so who cares. "Those hicks don't mind," will be the cry; "they're used to bad treatment."

A groundswell will finally inform people where West Virginia is and of the deplorable conditions in some of the communities. The nation's collective shame will be redeemed when it insists that some of West Virginia's coal money be used to pay for running water, sewage, better schools and better paying jobs.

And don't forget the state pension funds that are so far in the red that the people were asked to dig into their own pockets to fund a bond. The Massey Coal Company CEO spent heavily to defeat the bond—some say in retaliation for the increased severance tax. He says it was for the best interest of the state. The people voted the bond down. He also spent thousands to defeat a judge not to his liking. Are judgeships for sale? What next? What should West Virginia do? Let Pennsylvania take the north, Virginia the Eastern Panhandle, Ohio can extend its valley, and the southern mountains can simply be fenced in with a sign "No admittance for 1,000 years." That's too easy. The hard reality is that the state has to get its budget under control.

On West Virginia's 50th birthday, the population was increasing, the education system was growing, newspapers were flourishing and the state was bustling. There was not only swelling pride in the relatively new state, but there was an abundance of natural wealth and resources, unknown anywhere else, that promised nothing but happiness and prosperity in the years to come—which became happiness and prosperity for the few who manipulated the laws. Of course it was during this time that land and mineral rights were taken on the cheap from innocent folk. That is where the irony and tragedy enter, not because the state has relied on the "extraction" industries, but because of a lack of the very leadership qualities that had been so prominent in the greatest struggle this country has known.

West Virginia's leadership, both government and corporate, must protect the interests of the people. West Virginia should be the pride and glory of the rest of the country. The current situation the state finds itself in begs the question: if coal and timber have been so good, why are things so bad? Mountaintop mining removal is mindless and heartless and is putting millions if not billions of dollars into corporate pocketbooks, leaving the southern portion of this state in utter annihilation both in terms of the land and its people. Meanwhile the state is in a constant state of insolvency. Things are bad today because of decades of corrupt politics and ineffectual leadership that failed to stand up and look out for the people's interests, leadership that in some instances did wrong and tolerated wrong.

If as a good-natured but serious friend said, "West Virginia needs all the help it can get," then every West Virginian's contribution is vital. We need leaders and volunteers in all areas. Is there a more appropriate time than today in West Virginia to be discussing leadership and the need for the kind of leadership that Abraham Lincoln practiced? Is Lincoln and leadership taught in any of the MBA programs today? What happened with the *New York Times*, the Catholic Church, Arthur Anderson, Enron, WorldCom, the mutual fund scandal, certain prominent sports figures, and the shameful behavior of any number of corporations and individuals is a lesson for leadership across this country. The dirt has been building up for decades. It will take a lot of cleansing, a lot of soul searching, and a lot of work to restore confidences that have been battered and brutalized.

It is hard to predict where this leadership will come from—perhaps Massey Coal's CEO. We are all potential leaders. Lincoln was the essence of leadership, and his lessons are invaluable. Lincoln was straightforward with no gimmicks—though one may certainly speculate over his handling of issuing the emancipation proclamation. Theodore Blegen in a wonderful slim volume of Lincoln's imagery writes,

> *Great leadership, in the democratic world [let us recall those "mountaineers" who shared a spirit, and a willingness to fight and thus not only attained statehood for West Virginia but helped save the union from dissolution and arguably saved democracy itself] –great leadership—is no trick of style, no device of words, no garment of rhetoric. It is mind and knowledge, character and experience, courage and devotion, oneness with the people, and a vision and imagination that rise above the torment and fray of the passing hour.*

Lincoln's intelligence was combined with courage, perseverance, and a passionate devotion to principle. He had his goals and a vision. He wanted to keep the union intact and in the end, I believe he wanted to get rid of slavery—all the more so as the war progressed. To a certain extent, he really did not know all that much about the institution of slavery at the start of his Presidency. If the defeat of slavery was not quick enough for some or if some feel Lincoln was a racist, they can probably find justification for that viewpoint. Lincoln was operating under intense pressure. But his way of dealing and coping, his ethics and his style of leadership—warts and all—should be required reading and study for all of us, especially for those in positions of leadership. None of us are immune from the pitfalls that have ensnared so many. We should look back to Lincoln and the frontier and remember the awful human cost that was paid for this place. It is too easy to forget who we are or what we were going to be. But Lincoln tells us. He was passionate in his beliefs, and his instructions for who we are as a people and as a country and where we needed to go are valued lessons for all—certainly for West Virginians.

Lincoln said he read aloud because it helped him think. Perhaps West Virginians need to read aloud. For his day Lincoln's height made him an especially commanding figure. This may have helped him a bit in his role as a leader. Perhaps our governors should put lifts in their shoes. Maybe the coal leaders will pay attention.

If we would study Lincoln in regard to leadership and dealing with people, it could help us on how to get along in the workplace, how to deal with people in a more open, more collaborative, more "equal" and fair way. Again, Lincoln was not infallible, and at times he was ruthless in trying to achieve his goals. He commented that the presidency was "no bed of roses;" said that he "didn't amount to pig tracks in the War Department;" said that he "had endured a great deal of ridicule without much malice, and received a great deal of kindness, not quite free from ridicule."[1] Sounds like a West Virginian to me. About General Fremont, Lincoln said; "His cardinal mistake is that he isolates himself, and allows nobody to see him; and by which he does not know what is going on in the very matter he is dealing with." Leaders must always get out among the people (Lincoln called those outings his "public opinion baths.")

Lincoln knew what was going on. He remarked on the willingness to hear bad news. It "reminds me of an old acquaintance who having a son of a scientific turn, bought him a microscope. The boy went around, experimenting with his glass upon everything. One day at the dinner table, his father took up a piece of cheese. "Don't eat that, father," said the boy; "it is full of wrigglers." "My son," replied the old gentleman, taking a huge bite, "Let 'em wriggle; I can stand it if they can." Today our leaders seem at times remarkably uninformed about what is going on in their companies. When you lose the confidence of those around you and under you, you have lost everything. When the people feel that nothing will come of yet another new study, credibility is hard to regain. They are tired of various "agencies" hearing their complaints and then doing nothing. The governor as the leader must instill trust in state government or else the people will simply continue to believe that government leaders are acting on behalf of friends and business partners and not the people.

West Virginia's Senator Robert C. Byrd is surely a Lincoln scholar. If West Virginia's greatest politician can fashion himself after Lincoln, then it might behoove other mountain leaders to do the same. Byrd, like Lincoln, understands power and the power of words more than any leader West Virginia has ever had. Byrd, like Lincoln, is a great "politicker." He has honed his public speaking and wit from the time he was a young man. He learned to work his stories and his metaphors, making them vivid and concrete so they would have the desired effect.

Lincoln could also talk to the people and with the people and not over their heads. He wasn't crazy about being labeled a "country bumpkin" by the eastern press. People made fun of his accent. West Virginians can appreciate these slights. Byrd, like Lincoln, at one time was a Washington outsider and always reminded West Virginians he was one of them. Indeed he is the son of a coal miner and the husband of a coal miner's daughter. Lincoln, while not fond of his "splitter of rails" image, used it to his advantage. Byrd has also embraced his background. "Common looking people are the best in the world. That is the reason the Lord makes so many of them."[2] This was a sentiment of Lincoln's that Byrd would readily agree with.

Though I may disagree with Byrd's stand on mountaintop mining, I do not doubt for a moment what he has meant for West Virginia, what he has meant for this nation. He is an icon of individuality whose name stands with Lincoln's in West Virginia's history—a book Byrd is still writing. He will, I feel, go down in history not only for his justifiable generosity to a state that has sacrificed more than its share of lives for the good of the nation—both in terms of serving our country in war and providing cheap energy—but for being one of the great and most eloquent senators who ever graced the Senate floor. There should be a statue of Senator Byrd in front of the Capitol in Charleston. Byrd has carried the state on his back for the last half century. The state could easily and justifiably be renamed for him.

At the time when people were rather amazed at the number of statues of the past leaders of Iraq, they might also be rather taken aback by the number of memorials dedicated to Senator Byrd in West Virginia. Byrd gets some flack for this, but he deserves every one of them. But Byrd's memorials were not erected out of fear of a dictator, but were gratefully erected with affection because no one has done more for West Virginia. Indeed Byrd is worthy of a statue in Statutory Hall in our nation's capital. Ironically, Byrd is in serious danger of losing his Senate seat because West Virginia is turning Republican.

West Virginians have endured hunger, fear, anger, and public humiliation through the media and exploitation. They constantly endure threats of job loss. They have faced obstacles that have threatened their very existence so many times that they think, "What's the use?" When all seemed lost, they had the healing of the trees and mountains. Now they are losing those. But time and again many West Virginians—like my grandparents, and my parents, and my in-laws—have risen above their fate. They, like others before them, called upon their religion, work ethic, humor, and family to carry them through. West Virginia needs leaders who will not only assert moral authority but will help our population attain opportunity and equality so the state can forge a path to economic and educational stability.

The early mountain men and women would not be slaves nor would they be masters. They did not submit. It is interesting that those early men who led the battle for western Virginia were not, in the main, politically savvy. They simply did what they were entitled to do. It was the case of the few and the many as one of the leaders W. T. Willey noted a century and a half ago. Power was in the hands of a few, as it is today. The question is, do we have the courage to stand up? Is there a revolt in the making? "With malice toward none; with charity for all; with firmness in the right, as God gives us to see the right, let us strive on to finish the work we are in; to bind up the nation's wounds; to care for him who shall have borne the battle, and for his widow, and his orphan— to do all which may achieve and cherish a just, and a lasting peace, among ourselves, and with all nations."

What Lincoln wrote was a "how to" manual on leadership in crisis. Government has, Lincoln said, a responsibility "to do for the people what they can not do at all, or well, for themselves." This is the kind of leadership West Virginia needs, the kind of governor it must have, the kind of governor who will fight power and privilege and special exceptions.

Politics is an honorable profession, but many West Virginians are skeptical about politicians—sometimes for good reason—but not skeptical enough to try and fully inform themselves of what is going on outside their immediate area. We mountaineers should take care to learn all we can about our state and not to hold anything back, to share the stories of our lives with those who want to hear them, to reach out to others. Each one of us has a unique story to tell. West Virginia meant so much to me that perhaps I placed too many expectations on it. I have maintained a proprietary and rooting interest for all things truly West Virginian.

West Virginia's avowed independence is somewhat compromised by a dependence on government jobs and government money—Senator Byrd's children—and by a lack of education. The "wild and wonderful" threatens to be no more than a wishful slogan of the tourism department if there is no backbone to stand up to those who want to destroy it. The more you look into this, the more complicated and unresolved it seems to get. But embracing the mountain state and knowing that we all share the struggle, that we are all full of contradictions and incompleteness, hopefully allows us to look for positive venues that will move us ahead.

We struggle together to find what we are supposed to be. That's what community is, not about each tending his or her own garden, but tending the co-operative garden where we all plant and reap for the common good, where we all understand our place in the grand scheme. In a country of individuals, we are now struggling to see how free we can truly be without destroying the whole. Mary Catherine Bateson writes hopefully:

> *We must transform our attitude toward all productive work and toward the planet into expressions of homemaking, where we create and sustain the possibility of life...the problem is with our understanding of the materialities that make life possible: the forest and the cooking pots, the necessary recuperation time of fields and workers, the private spaces of our lives where the spirit flourishes, and the woodlands that are still wild.*[3]

People are more aware today about conserving energy and water, about recycling, about cutting down on waste. West Virginia University has taken a leading role in organic farming. It is launching a sorely needed study of water and land management issues. There are some very good facilities in the state researching energy for the future. New environmental technologies are being studied. Research and development hold the promise of more jobs in a state that sorely needs more jobs. Manufacturers can prevail when faced with technical problems. Industry can and has come a long way toward combating smog. The Japanese are building sixty miles-to-the-gallon cars. We have pollution-free paint. Perhaps we can burn clean coal at some point.

What we don't seem to be able to do is treat the land and people with consistent respect and fairness. It took millions of years for the southern Appalachian Mountains to be formed and just a blink of an eye for them to be gone. We might as well take a limb from every citizen. We all need to be in touch with that part of our being that Robert Bly writes about in *Iron John, the Wild Man*.

> *When the Wild Man has been preserved inside, a man also feels a genuine friendliness toward the wilderness in nature." We need to remember the Wild Man and the Wild Woman because "men and women need now, more than ever in history, to protect the earth, its creatures, the waters, the air, the mountains, the trees, the wilderness.*

In West Virginia in the early 1900s, coal, oil, gas and lumber were thought to have brought unbounded wealth to West Virginia. It should rival other states in material advancement and prosperity. It is no exaggeration to say there should be no poverty. One would think that the amount of coal in the hills of West Virginia would have guaranteed economic salvation for the people, but coal has had a perverse effect on politics and economic development. What coal has meant for West Virginia is what oil has meant for Iraq: authoritarianism, corruption, and economic stagnation. To move forward we need a comprehensive statewide plan for the land and its resources. We the people need to assume responsibility. That is what life asks. Then there is the problem: what to do? The answer begins with each of us doing our best, becoming informed and voting. It doesn't matter so much what side of the political fence you are on—just vote.

When people submit fraudulent claims for worker's compensation, they are abdicating responsibility. Worker's compensation is $3.6 billion in debt. People know that claimants almost always win. Some say that coal companies underpaid premiums for years or went bankrupt to avoid paying, so why not file. People think the companies cheat, that politicians cheat, so why shouldn't they cheat? It's free money, like hitting the lottery. One wrong, of course, does not justify another.

A West Virginia company can save money by moving to Virginia. Worker's compensation has been under funded and in the hole from the beginning. Everybody blames everybody else. The governor needs to build relationships with the legislature so that together they say, "Stop arguing and fix it or scrap it and start all over." The governor's challenges are admittedly enormous at a time when West Virginia's economy is projected to grow at only a snail's pace, with jobs being lost in mining and manufacturing.

West Virginia is pretty much off the radar screen for companies wanting to relocate. The perception is that West Virginia offers an unfavorable climate for business with high taxes and uncontrolled lawsuits. The state can't afford to or doesn't offer incentives to companies to locate here. When I asked a company to consider filming in West Virginia, I was told if West Virginia would offer some sort of rebate, it would be considered. The company was told West Virginia did not have incentive packages—period, end of discussion. Missouri did, and that is where the company went. One can look at incentives as a form of blackmail, but several states now have packages in place. They are trying to attract business that is currently going to Canada and Australia. Image is another problem. West Virginia is considered an isolated, poor, coal-unionized state.

But that perception is wrong. When I grew up in West Virginia, I never knew any hillbillies or rednecks or hayseeds. I went to high school with future CEO's and college presidents, judges and lawyers, doctors, teachers, generals, journalists, real estate moguls, writers, pilots, coaches, editors, publishers, designers, carpenters, electricians, plumbers, mechanics, coal miners—even actors. I was delighted to be from West Virginia, but then I was a product of the fifties, when to my eyes everything looked rosy. Elvis was king and making a living was possible. But it wasn't really possible for all in West Virginia, and that's why so many people left in the fifties. In the sixties birth control pills became a reality, racial unrest was simmering and the quagmire of Vietnam was about to deepen. But I had found the girl of my dreams. She was indeed "my bridge over troubled water."

We need to instill in West Virginian's children the strength, courage, fortitude and commitment that the state's forefathers had in fighting for statehood, a place they thought they could call their own, home. Home is more than a place, more than oneness with the land. Home is within us, and it comes to be when we reach out to touch those around us, reach out to the deepest hollow, bringing us all together within the circle of family. It is this connection that leads us to wholeness. It is this wholeness that we must instill, as mentors, in the children of West Virginia. This will require time, sacrifice, patience, work, and an abundance of grace and love to ensure that the wants and dreams of West Virginia's children and its people can be fulfilled.

This will also require jobs. If our ancestors could help eliminate the greatest challenge this country has ever faced—slavery—then surely we can lick the current problems of West Virginia and thus help ourselves. People must choose, and this involves risk, faith, and a trust that understanding will come. West Virginia must decide what it wants and be willing to suffer the bumps along the road. It will cost time and money, but in the end West Virginia will be enhanced a hundredfold.

We need a statewide group of mentors who will directly interact with young people across the state. The idea of mentors is to help the young people do what they cannot do for themselves. It brings to mind the nature of West Virginia. West Virginia has always suffered from a weak economy, and there are several reasons and plenty of blame to go around. But we must move beyond assigning blame.

What can be done to encourage the young technological wizards to continue experimenting with new uses for coal besides burning? The governor should consider forming a non-partisan commission whose only agenda is to identify problems and make recommendations as to what should be done to make West Virginia better. Then the governor must use his position as a bully pulpit to help get the commission's report enacted. Mountaineers must demand more from their leaders, more openness, more transparency, more equality, more accessibility, more willingness to go out among the people and explain to them his or her vision. Lincoln held that the Civil War was "essentially a people's contest." We must insist; it is imperative that government does as Lincoln said it must: "elevate the condition of men—to afford all, an unfettered start, and a fair chance, in the race of life." They are just words, but they are words that form the basis of this country's foundation.

West Virginians on the whole have had to struggle to keep body and soul together without having to worry about reclaiming responsibilities. They are burdened with responsibilities as it is. An unemployed miner with time on his hands and no future needs encouragement and the opportunity to be retrained for employment. He needs help finding that old spring in his walk. There was never much concern about keeping up with the Joneses in West Virginia because most everyone was in the same boat. If things are bad in the rest of the country, a West Virginian thinks, "What's the big deal," because things are usually bad for most folks in West Virginia. Business is always "about the same." The people have been taken advantage of by both outsiders and locals. But it hurts even more when an exploiter is homegrown—

those who have preyed on the natural wealth of their state without feeling the slightest obligation to give back. It is absolutely a requirement to give back. A governor has to convey this, has to make it understandable why it is necessary to give back.

There is a good-sized reserve of coal. Can the governor get the people's rightful share? The governor is the hub of the wheel. It is the governor and not the members of the United States Congress who is closest to the people. The governor knows or should know the realities of life for the people. Corporate interests, political groups, and labor unions all have had a hand in what has been a sorry story for the people. One can hope that individual state legislators have executed the wishes of the people they represent, but have they? This play has many players.

West Virginia for all its aversion to big government and its romantic ties to frontier independence and individuality has grown to depend on "Byrd droppings." His "dropping" of the FBI and NASA centers has helped spearhead a high tech corridor along Interstate 79 that holds much promise for the future of mountaineers. West Virginia has to nurture other resources. The governor needs to look at other states and see what they are doing right. West Virginia can, in time, turn the corner in migration reversal. Hopefully city people will migrate outward in increasing numbers as they discover the ease and attributes of a simpler existence: faith, work, community, and family.

Then, as in the Eastern Panhandle, the problem will be how to control growth. In some ways I feel the north and the Eastern Panhandle and the south of West Virginia act not like a family today, but rather like divorcees. They cannot divide themselves into areas of sectional pride any longer. The Eastern Panhandle, the Ohio River Valley, the Mountain area, and the coalfields must truly unite for a "one for all and all for one" mentality. McDowell and other southern counties seem like poor orphans. When funds are tight, we need to be watchful of the "what's in it for us" way of portioning out state monies. Perhaps, as has been suggested, some counties can be consolidated. Perhaps the two major universities can work together to avoid duplicating disciplines.

If things are progressing in the northern sections or in the Eastern Panhandle, let us see how we can work together to encourage small business and entrepreneurs to help bring progress to all of the state, remembering what Lincoln said about a house divided—"it will become all one thing, or all the other." With that in mind, let us also recall "the better angels of our nature." Let's communicate and share ideas and form cooperative ventures to retrain the work force. What are venture capitalists and the banks doing in terms of West Virginia's development? What happened to the "Shared Vision" that was touted a few years ago? We need to link the educational outlets with the latest technology to make sure every person is reached. Our colleges and universities must be tapped more fully for their research potential and as centers for economic and cultural development. They could also recommend how the number of state employees might be reduced. They could do a joint study of the state constitution to see if it needs amending.

West Virginia is rightfully proud of the positive and good things of its past. Barbara Freese wrote, "Whether we and the people who will follow us remember coal for the way it helped build our civilization or the way it helped undermine it depends—as so many more important things do—on the climate ahead."[4] What we know of the future can help us make policy today. There is still a way to right wrongs. This is not the last of times. Many periods have been marked by devastation. Of course technology has increased the potential for devastation. Thornton Wilder at the end of *The Skin Of Our Teeth* writes,

> *The whole world's at sixes and sevens, and why the house hasn't fallen down about our ears long ago is a miracle to me.... Mr. and Mrs. Antrobus! Their heads are full of plans and they're confident as the first day they began.*[5]

West Virginians need to be as confident and hopeful as West Virginians were on that first euphoric day of independence from Virginia. There lies the rub, if history has taught us anything. West Virginians need to be careful about that elation called euphoria, remembering to temper it with a hard-nosed diligence that holds their leaders accountable.

As we have seen, nothing brings people to rediscover their

country or mountain more than when the loss of that country or mountain is threatened. There are many things in this often harsh, hard world that one doesn't agree with, but you find a way to work, to adapt, because of the inherent greater good that will find its way. I don't believe that anyone thinks that blowing up mountains is a good thing to do—including Massey's CEO. It's the old argument that the ends justify the means. West Virginia is at what Thoreau called the "hard bottom." It is here where we can share with each other, take time with each other, as we ponder and try to combat the two tons of toxic waste that is produced for every man, woman and child. In the conclusion of *The Time of Man*, Elizabeth Maddox Roberts wrote, "Where are we a-goin, Mammy?' Nan said. 'I don't know. Somewheres... Some better place,' Hen said."

On our open porch as a teenager, I would lie in the sun and dream. I was a rower on a rolling sea of hills. Having no destination, I found another hill child, and together we rode the waves down to other shores. We have been schooled and have some experience of the world, and understand that relationships within the world are complex. We want to go forward with the rest of our nation with a mother's arm gently but firmly nudging us on to a greater understanding that will make a better home, a home that is not at the expense of another. I have traveled beyond my wildest dreams. Only minutes after crossing the state line all things West Virginian begin to wash over me: the insecurities, prejudices, inadequacies, attitudes, the innocence, the independence, the likes and dislikes, the smell of a fall football game, the sense of humor, the spirit, the people, and on and on even to the point of singing John Denver's *Country Roads* as I drive those mountain roads. But West Virginia will sing best if all West Virginians have a chance to sing as one big chorus. When that happens, West Virginia will have a strong and enduring foundation for the future.

Family will be the key to any new foundation. My oldest daughter works in a hospital and sees the stark loneliness of those without family. People do not like to be lonely, but family makes the loneliness bearable. My daughter says that family is everything. She is right, though sometimes we get so consumed with work that we seemingly have little need or time for intimate personal relationships. September 11th tragically reminded us of our obligation to our fellow man and to family. From Iraq and other wars we have heard and read the stories of lives lost. We have also seen the diversity of people on both sides whose common bond was family, held together by love and grace.

We have witnessed hero after hero being memorialized. We have seen leaders emerge. I know that my father's generation of World War II has justly been called the "great generation," but the individuals, civilian and soldier alike, that we have mourned and saluted after September 11 do not take a backseat to anyone. The true heroes are not in films and novels; they are standing beside us, and the image of the American man and woman—not withstanding the Iraq prison abuse—is one our children can look up to.

Family and theatre, though I never saw them coming, were blessed happenstances, and they have given me whatever little wisdom I possess, along with whatever humanity. It is family that has sustained me, helped me to open my mind to what is in front of me, to strengthen me and open the window of possibilities. It is family that has given me balance, a desire for exactness, not perfection, but to see things with more preciseness. Family has also given me courage and a reason to go on. September 11th, rather than stifling life, has forced me to reassess, to see as never before that a good family is like a clear day where you can see forever.

My father has never stopped saying, "When are you coming home? Don't forget where I live." I might ask the same of my children. But home, I have learned, is more than a place, more than oneness with land. Home is within us, and it comes to be when we reach out to touch those around us, bringing together a circle of family. This requires time, sacrifice, patience, work, forgiveness, and an abundance of grace and love. This is what my wife and children have taught me.

We must work harder to learn about each other, about our places, in order to have a better chance of bringing each into the circle of home. Many people since 9-11 have taken stock of their lives. There comes a time, whether young or old, to evaluate where you are, how your life is shaping up, and no one can answer for you. You and only you will choose how to live your life. Facing your own destiny is what ambition is about.

My own children have at times moved with a degree of uncertainty, but they are going forward in a world much more dangerous and unpredictable than it was when I was young. In this uncertain world, part of me wants my children to stay home. Yet I know that for them to find their home, they must follow their individual path, paths that could conceal land mines not of their doing. It is such a cruel violation to the innocent searches of the young as they go about seeking their desires. All we can do for our children is to ask a question here and there to perhaps make them more aware of what their decisions involve. Perhaps the best thing is to give our children hugs and open the door for them, as my mother did for me.

Where is the light? It will be in the ideas that we pass on to our children, the ideas that they pass on to our grandchildren. It is the family unit that fosters and mentors foundations of grace and love.

West Virginia is where I came from, where I used to belong. It is still there for me. It will always welcome me back. It has drawn me back to look at my life, where I am, where I have been, who I am, what I am—a sort of retrospection that might tell me where I am going. It has bid me to look back and to look in the mirror—something I have avoided except for reasons of vanity—and try and see and hopefully understand a little better the person looking back at me. Thoreau's *Walden* reverberates today, when we all yearn for a secret place, a retreat from the world. I need my pick-me-up visits to the hills, ever returning to where I came from. People in those hills have good advice to offer.

My wife and I wanted to stay close to our children, and their lives are now in California. So that is where we'll stay. While all West Virginians know about California, but not very many Californians know anything about West Virginia. I consider myself lucky, so I will tell all about that special place.

POSTSCRIPT

In June of 2005, my wife and I sold our house. This was both freeing and emotionally difficult. Our children are grown, and enchanting as our house was and as fond and attached to it as we were for twenty years, it was a place we realized we could walk away from, because a house is not a home. At this same time, we most happily traded in our SUV for a hybrid car that gets very good gas mileage—it is a Japanese car. With gas prices as high as they are, and rising every day it seems, I had no guilt whatsoever about buying a foreign car. Americans are flooding Toyota showrooms as General Motors—now that the horse is long out of the barn—finally realizes they are going to get hammered. Perhaps the governor can persuade Toyota to build the Prius car at its plant in West Virginia.

My father has moved to a very nice assisted living home. His house just got too lonely by himself. The move for Dad was wrenching, but soon he found that his life still had value and that was a blessing. It was restoring. He looks forward to the communal meals and outings. To be accepted and appreciated is to be found, to be given a home. Dad has a new home where each member has a distinct identity, and each one is important for the survival of the whole.

Life is fragile. It is not permanent, none of it. We must all get used to change. God bless West Virginia.

NOTES AND SOURCES

The writer, a native West Virginian, has been a life long reader of anything having to do with West Virginia, specifically, and Appalachia in general. The poetry of Louise McNeil and Muriel Dressler; the stories of Mary Lee Settle, Denise Giardina, and Breece D'J Pancake; the publications *Goldenseal, Wonderful West Virginia* and Jim Comstock's (no one loved West Virginia more) *West Virginia Hillbilly* are many of the regional publications he treasures.

The writer's love of Abraham Lincoln started in his days of graduate school in Illinois, where as an actor he took on the first of many roles as Lincoln. Many books and numerous articles about Lincoln were researched in preparation for his play, *Lincoln and James*. Another play, *Final Assault*, a story about a woman trying to save her mountain, gave the writer the pleasure to research another beloved subject: West Virginia.

David Selby is indebted to his many friends in West Virginia for their free flowing conversations through the years about a place they all love. Some of those conversations have made it into this book in one fashion or another. Selby has written this book over the course of several years. While every attempt has been made to footnote and appropriately credit specific sources, sometimes this was not possible. Much of the data and many of the statistics were obtained from the Internet, and he has cited specific websites for your reference in the endnotes. Two frequent sources were *The Charleston Gazette* and the *Charleston Daily Mail*.

Prologue: My Trip to the Mountains

[1] Selby, Clyde. *My Trip To The Mountains*. My father wrote this report in 1932 at the age of 16 for the Trail Blazers Club.

Chapter 1: Gardeners

[1] Basler, Roy. *The Collected Works Of Abraham Lincoln*, New Brunswick, NJ: Rutgers University Press, 1953.
[2] Lowell, James Russell. *Democracy*, New York: P.F. Collier & Son, 1938. p. 450.
[3] "Exodus of Young Adults Getting Worse." Huntington, WV: *Herald Dispatch*. Apr. 28, 2002.
[4] Gaouette, Nicole. "Illegal Population Flows to Southwest," *LA Times*. June 15, 2005, sec. A, p. 13.

Chapter 2: The Lessons of 9-11

[1] Locke, Louis, edited by. "Toward a Definition of Tolerance," from *Toward a Liberal Education*. Austin, TX: Holt, Rinehart and Winston, 1989. p. 692.
[2] Lowell, *Democracy*, p. 455.
[3] Dillard, Annie. "Total Eclipse," from *Best American Essays*. Boston: Houghton Mifflin Co., 2000. p. 487.
[4] Dideon, Joan. "*The White Album*," from *Best American Essays*. Boston: Houghton Mifflin Co., 2000. p. 421.
[5] Tillich, Paul. *The Courage To Be*, New Haven, CT: Yale University Press, 1952. p. 107.
[6] MacLeish, Archibald. "Epistle to Be Left in the Earth," from *Collected Poems of Archibald MacLeish*, Boston: Houghton Mifflin Co., 1962.
[7] Tillich, *The Courage To Be*.
[8] Locke, Louis. *Toward a Liberal Education*. p. 404.
[9] Dovey, Kimberly. Quoted by Clare Cooper Marcus, *House As A Mirror Of Self*. Berkeley, CA: Conari Press, 1995. p. 191.
[10] Dunaway, David K. *Huxley In Hollywood*, New York: Harper and Row, 1989. p. 392.
[11] Lowell, *Democracy*, p. 455.
[12] Thoreau, Henry David. "Where I Lived, and What I Lived For," from *Modern Essays In English*, ed. by Joseph Frank. Boston: Little, Brown and Co., 1966. p. 423.
[13] Sevaried, Eric. "*The Dark Of The Moon*," from *Reading for Rhetoric*. New York: Macmillan, 1962. p. 451.

Chapter 3: Homeland

[1] Foster, Ruel E. *Pictures From An Institution, from West Virginia University*, Louisville, KY: Harmony House, 1987.
[2] Stegner, *Marking The Sparrow's Fall*, New York: Henry Holt and Company, 1998. p.5.
[3] Basler, *The Collected Works of Abraham Lincoln*, Vol. 4. p. 203.
[4] Cuomo, Mario. *Why Lincoln Matters*, New York: Harcourt, Inc., 2004. p. 30.
[5] Basler, *The Collected Works Of Abraham Lincoln*, Vol. 3. p. 315.

⁶ Anderson, L.T. editorial in the *Charleston (WV) Gazette*. Feb. 14, 1979.

Chapter 4: Mountaineers
¹ Russell, Donna. *Selby Families of Colonial America*, New Market, MD: Catoctin Press, 1990.
² Stegner, Wallace. *Marking The Sparrow's Fall*, p. 200.
³ Furbee, Mary R. "Mountaineer Emeritus." Charleston, WV: *Goldenseal*, Fall 1996. p.34.
⁴ Carson, Rachel. "The Marginal World," from *Best American Essays*. Boston: Houghton Mifflin Co., 2000. p. 214.
⁵ Schlesinger, Arthur. "The Crises Of American Masculinity" from *Reading for Rhetoric*, New York: Macmillan Co, 1962. p. 298.
⁶ McElhinny, Brad. "West Virginians and War," *Charleston (WV) Daily Mail*. Nov. 8, 1999.
⁷ Kriesky, Jill. "Prison System is Mortgaging State's Educational Future," Editorial on the Wheeling Jesuit University website at www.wju.edu. Feb. 17, 2005.
⁸ "Controversy Regarding OxyContin," from the American Society of Interventional Pain Physicians website at www.ASIPP.org
⁹ Lipton, Michael. "*Moon* Provoked Remarks In 1963," *Charleston (WV) Sunday Gazette*, June 20, 1993. p.2E.

Chapter 6: West Virginia Moon Revisted

¹ Rasmussen. Barbara. *Absentee Landowning and Exploitation in West Virginia, 1760-1920*, Lexington: University Press of Kentucky, 1994. p. 10
² Dressler, Muriel Miller. *Appalachia*. MHC Publications, 1977.

Chapter 7: Mountains of Coal

¹ Leopold, Aldo. *A Sand County Almanac*, New York: Oxford University Press, 1949. p. 223.
² Stockman, Vivian. "Mountaintop Removal Pits Miners vs. Townspeople," From the website for the *Progressive Populist* at http://www.populist.com/99.14.mountaintop.html
³ McTeer, J. David & Thomas N. Bethell. "Coal: Planning Its Future and Its Legacy," Wheeling Jesuit Univ. website at http://64.70.252.93/newfiles/Final_Report/IV_Supply/IV.2.b-Coal-PlanningitsFut.pdf
⁴ Letter written by Larry Gibson to the author, Nov. 25, 2004.
⁵ Basler, *Collected Works of Lincoln*, Vol. 7, p. 512.
⁶ Stockman, Vivian. "Mountaintop Removal Pits Miners vs. Townspeople."
⁷ Ward, Ken Jr., "Far From the Main Goal," *The Charleston (WV) Gazette*. Aug. 15, 2004.
⁸ Drew, Christopher and Richard A. Oppel, Jr. "Friends in White House Come to Coal's Aid," *New York Times*. Aug. 9, 2004.
⁹ McTeer, J. David & Thomas N. Bethell. "Coal: Planning Its Future and Its Legacy."
¹⁰ Caudill, Harry M. *Night Comes to The Cumberlands,* Boston: Little, Brown and Company, 1962.

[11] Taken from the website West Virginia Coal Facts at www.wvminesafety.org/wvcoalfacts.htm
[12] Murello, Carol. "Mining Town Rises in Anger," *Washington Post*. Jan. 6, 2005. sec B, p. 9.
[13] "Mercury Rising," from the National Campaign Against Dirty Air website http://cta.policy.net/ West Virginia is among the worst five states for electric utility mercury and toxic emissions.
[14] Newberry, Beth. "Mountain Defenders," Washington, DC: *Sojourners* Magazine. March 2005.
[15] Orwell, George. "Marrakech" from *Reading for Rhetoric*, New York: The Macmillan Company, 1962. p. 386.
[16] Kahn, Joseph. "China's Coal Mines Risk Danger For a Better Wage," *LA Times*. Jan. 28, 2003. sec. A, p. 3.
[17] Kriesky, Jill. "Prison System is Mortgaging State's Educational Future," Editorial from the Wheeling Jesuit University website www.wju.edu
[18] Lewis, Ronald. *Transforming the Appalachian Countryside*, Chapel Hill: The University of North Carolina Press, 1998.
[19] *Ibid.*
[20] "Timber Severance Tax Bill," from Sierra Club's website www.sierraclub.org Timber was trying to get its tax lowered from its already low rate of 3.2%. Governor Manchin vetoed the bill. That was a responsible decision. He is to be congratulated.
[21] "West Virginia: Economic Activities," from the MSN Encarta website http://encarta.msn.com/
[22] Stegner. *Marking The Sparrow's Fall*.
[23] Letter from Helen Pancake to the author, 1988.
[24] Stegner. *Marking The Sparrow's Fall*.
[25] Russell, Scott. *Writing From the Center*, Bloomington: Indiana University Press. 1995.

Chapter 8: Those Damn Facts and Figures

[1] Oberhauser, Ann M., Lillian J. Waugh, and Chris Weiss. "Gender Analysis and Economic Development in West Virginia," http://www.polsci.wvu.edu/ipa/par/report_13_2.html
[2] Moss, Jim. "Most Undereducated State in the Nation," Huntington, WV: *Herald-Dispatch*, July 11, 2004.
[3] Center For Tobacco Cessation website at http://ctcinfo.org/policy/fs/wv-ctcfacts.PDF
[4] Taken from the website for Social Security Essentials website at www.epinet.org/newsroom/releases/2005/socsecfactsheets/West_Virginia.pdf
[5] From the Tax Foundation website at http://www.taxfoundation.org

Chapter 9: Hometown

[1] Bassler, Collected Works of A. Lincoln, Vol. 3, p. 477.
[2] Bassler, Collected Works of A. Lincoln, Vol. 8, p. 170.
[3] Jung, C.G. *Memories, Dreams, Reflections*, New York: Vintage Books, 1961.
[4] "Levi Strauss Closes Last Two Plants," from www.CNN.com Jan. 8, 2004.

Chapter 11: The Carpenter

[1] Vidal, Gore. "Love of Flying," from *The New York Times Review of Books, 1963-93*, p. 270.
[2] Brooks, Van Wyck Brooks. "The Silent Generation," from *Reading for Rhetoric*. New York: McMillan Company, 1962. p.171.
[3] Oates, Joyce Carol Oates. "They All Just Went Away," from *Best American Essays*. Boston: Houghton Mifflin Co., 2000. p. 553
[4] Thoreau, Henry David. *Walking*. P.F. Collier & Son, 1938. p. 424.

Chapter 13: The Other Side of the Mountain

[1] Tillich. *The Courage To Be*.
[2] McPherson, James Allen. From the forward to *The Stories of Breece D'J Pancake*, Boston: Little Brown, 1983.
[3] Ellis, Alice Thomas. *A Welsh Childhood*, Pleasantville, NY: The Akadine Press, 1997.

Chapter 14: Looking Ahead

[1] Basler, *The Collected Works of Abraham Lincoln*, Vol. 6. p. 559.
[2] Hay, John. *Lincoln and the Civil War in the Diaries and Letter of John Hay*, New York: DaCapo Press, 1988. p. 143.
[3] Bateson, Mary Catherine. *Composing a Life,* New York: Atlantic Monthly Press, 1989.
[4] Freese, Barbara. Coal: A Human History, Cambridge, MA: Perseus Books. 2002.
[5] Wilder, Thornton. *Three Plays*, New York: Bantam Books. 1966.

ABOUT THE AUTHOR

David Selby has had a long, distinguished career on stage and in film and television. He is probably best known for his starring roles as Quentin Collins on the television series *Dark Shadows* and Richard Channing on *Falcon Crest*. He is the author of several plays and screenplays and has published three books. He and his wife are native West Virginians—he is from Morgantown—she from Beckley. They and their three children currently live in California.

It has been nearly forty years since Selby and his wife left West Virginia, and forty years since Harry Caudill wrote *Night Comes To The Cumberlands*. But Selby's feelings for the state are echoed in the words of Helen Pancake, mother of distinguished West Virginia writer, Breece D'J Pancake: "I'm more of a West Virginian now than I was the sixty-three years I lived there."